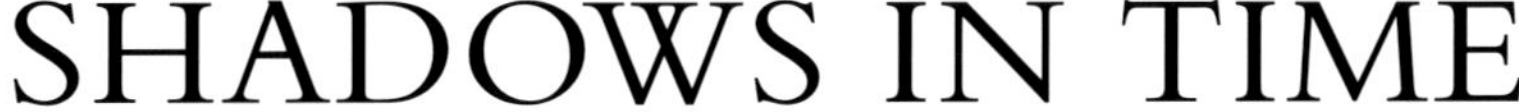
SHADOWS IN TIME

For all who tread lightly
on our fragile earth

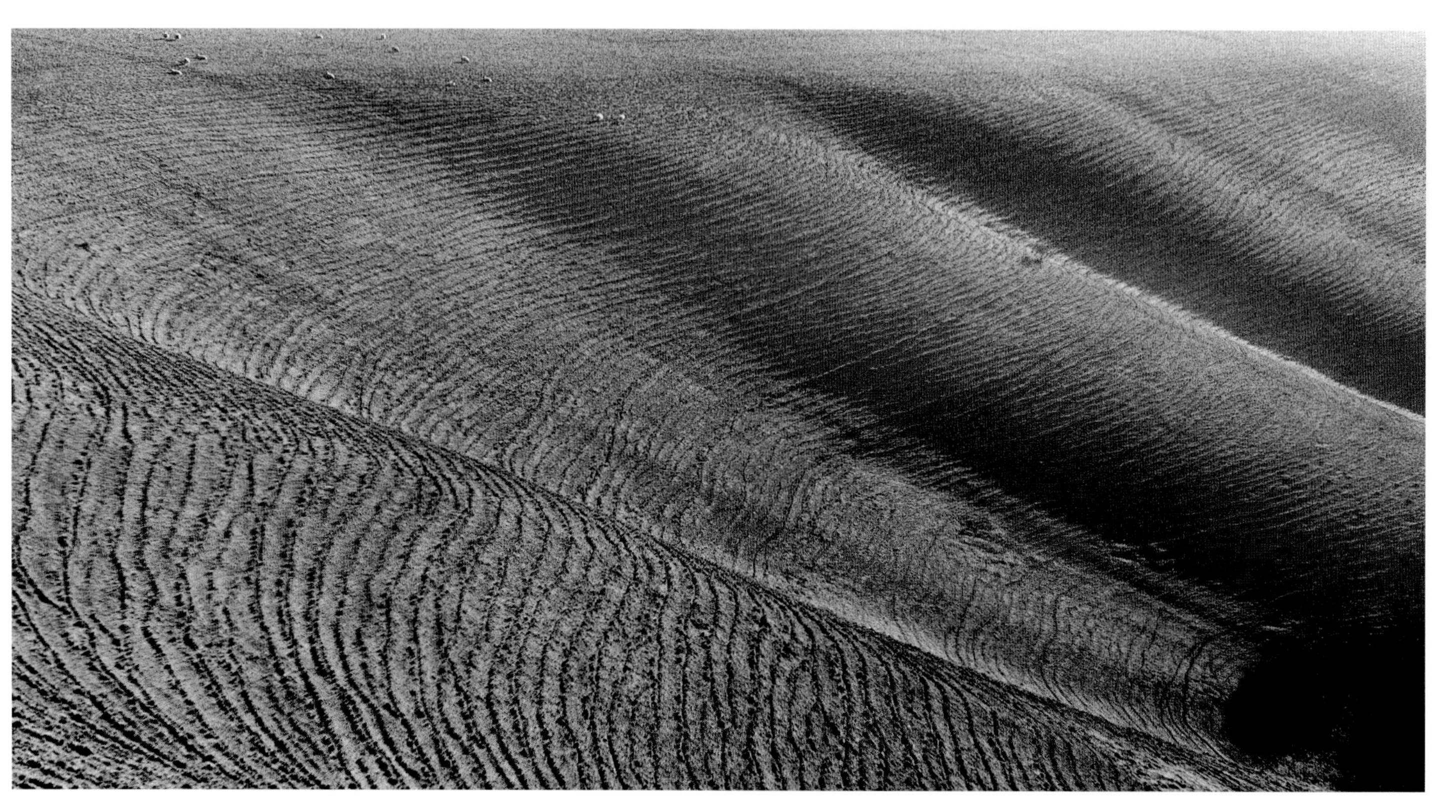

SHADOWS IN TIME

Images from the West Country

THE WORK OF FORTY WEST COUNTRY PHOTOGRAPHERS

Ron Frampton

An edition limited to 1,200 copies

CHURCHILL PUBLISHING
Devon · England

First published in 2002 by
Churchill Publishing, Devon, England

Designed by Ron Frampton

First Impression

A CIP catalogue record for this title
is available from the British Library

ISBN 0-9543170-0-9

CONTENTS

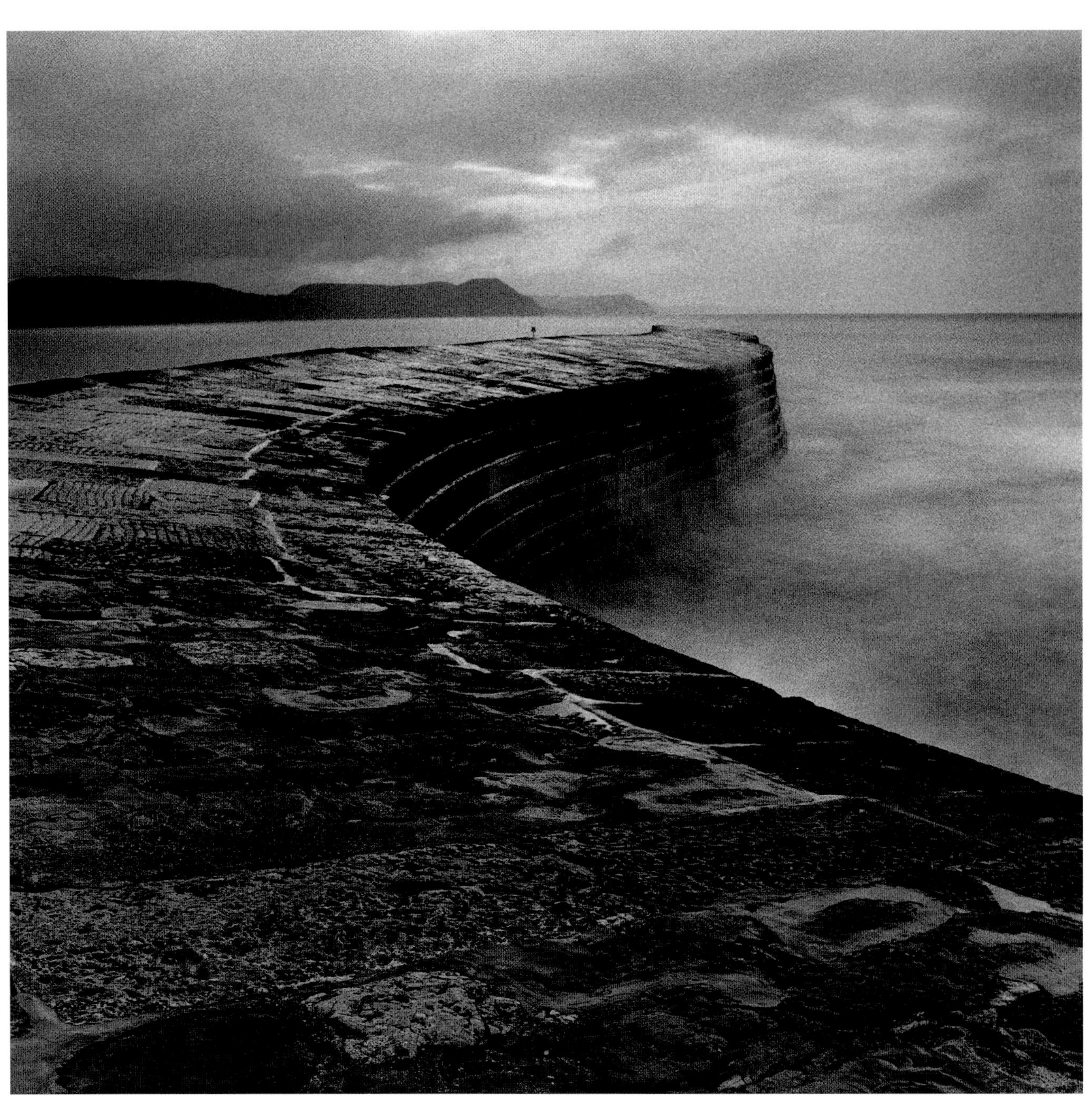

Crabbing

The sun just risen, the moon still high,
And nothing but the morning's birds,
The gulls, the redshanks, razorbills
Beneath the pale young summer sky–

These birds, the windless air and sea:
Quicky, his mate, my nephew and I
Chug westward to the wooded shore
In outward peace and honesty.

We stop and start and slowly haul
The wicker pots. Upward they float
Ribbed from the sea's translucent depths.
Hove on the deck the brown crabs crawl

Each osier cell. Then Quicky's skill:
Catching them neatly through the mouth,
The massive claws bent back just so,
He nicks and cuts. They soon lie still,

Baffled by all this light and death,
Ligaments severed, pincers vain.
I watch my nephew's knife-fixed stare,
His six-years-old of bated breath

As each spiked monster joins the rest.
He may relive them in his dreams,
As I did once, and wake one night
To face his sanity's first test

As scuttling horrors throng his bed.
I dreamt this many times when young:
That I was drowned, the world was drowned,
Only my flesh and the crabs not dead.

I touch his hair, but not for that.
I think how he, when he is old,
Will make a bitter judgement throne
Of this benched gunwale where he sat,

Since time must teach him that this dawn
Held something that we hid from him:
How his had been a shadowed year
In which no lucky child was born.

He must remember us with rage,
We three men on a dying sea
Who saw the oil and slicks of scum,
All the foul poison of their age

Filmed out around them like a pus,
Yet told him why the crabs got caught
Was out of stupid greed for bait.
We said they hadn't brains, like us.

Today he nods, and takes our word –
But what will he do when he looks back
And sees how cancerous-blind we were,
How sick, how viciously absurd?

Greed never trapped us in its cage.
We never sat and watched time haul
Earth onward to its stifled end.
He *must* remember us with rage.

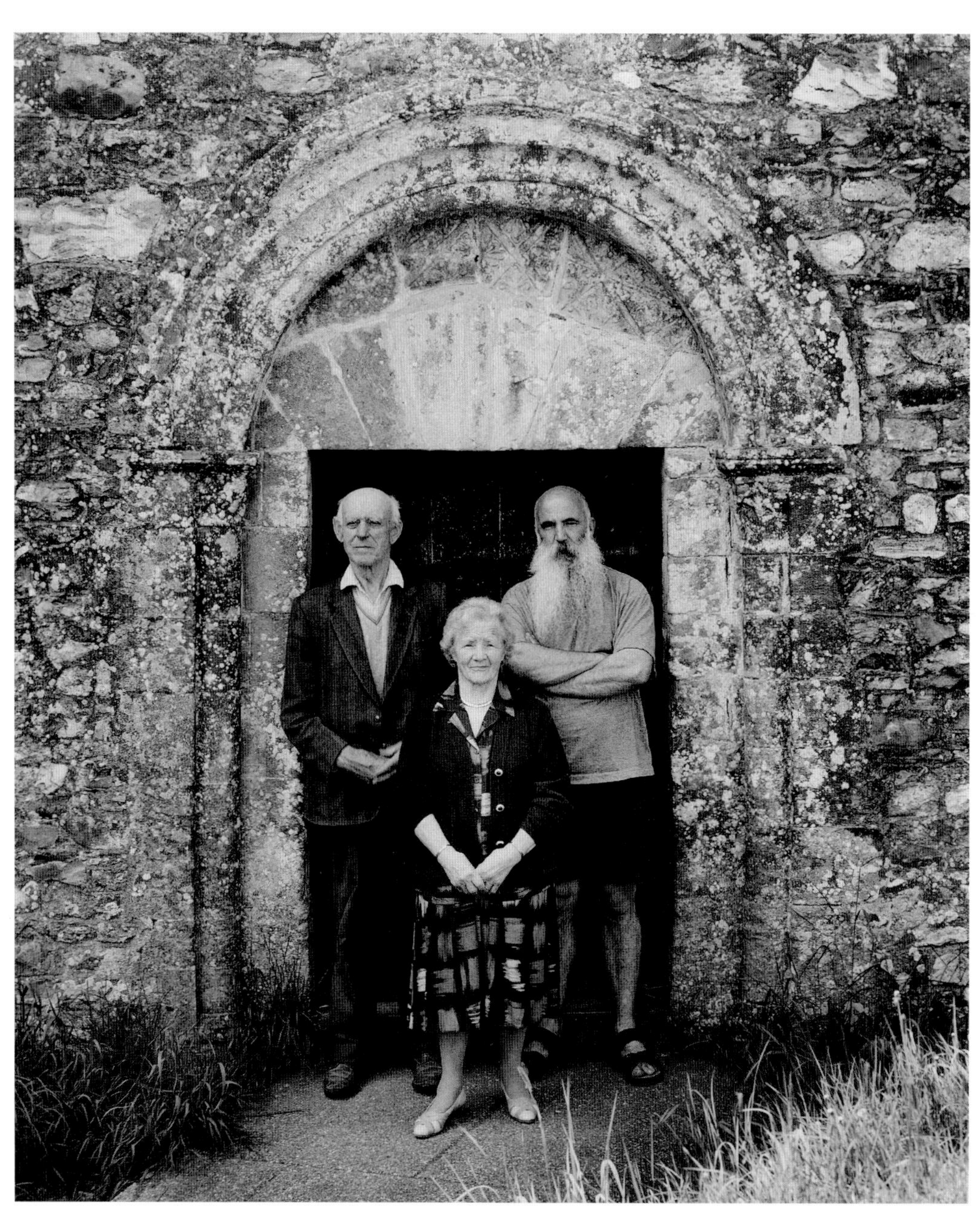

Donald Wyatt, Philip Thomason and Peggy Wyatt, St Michael, Cudworth, Somerset by Ulick Palmer

CONTRIBUTING PHOTOGRAPHERS

Stan Ashcroft, *Devon*

Ian Beech, *Somerset*

Richard Bland, *Somerset*

Janet Carmichael, *Devon*

Kirsten Cooke, *Dorset*

Dianne Dowling, *Devon*

Rob Dyson, *Dorset*

Pat Garth, *Somerset*

Nathan Glover, *Devon*

Carol Green, *Devon*

Natasha Greig, *Somerset*

Gordon Hall, *Somerset*

Paul Harvey, *Somerset*

Maisie Hill, *Dorset*

Peter Hill, *Somerset*

Richard Lane, *Dorset*

Peter Livingstone, *Somerset*

Michael Mammatt, *Somerset*

Katia Marsh, *Dorset*

Robin Mills, *Dorset*

Sue Milverton, *Somerset*

Jerry Mitchell, *Somerset*

John Nicholson, *Somerset*

Justin Orwin, *Somerset*

Denise Owen, *Somerset*

Ulick Palmer, *Somerset*

Liz Perry, *Somerset*

Christopher Rimmer, *Somerset*

Pauline Rook, *Somerset*

Nicky Saunter, *Devon*

Gerald Singleton, *Somerset*

Keith Smith, *Devon*

Brian Smyth, *Devon*

Paul Taylor, *Devon*

Vicky Taylor, *Somerset*

Abbey Thresher, *Somerset*

Adrian Turton, *Devon*

Emma Weal, *Devon*

Vicky West, *Devon*

Bob Williams, *Devon*

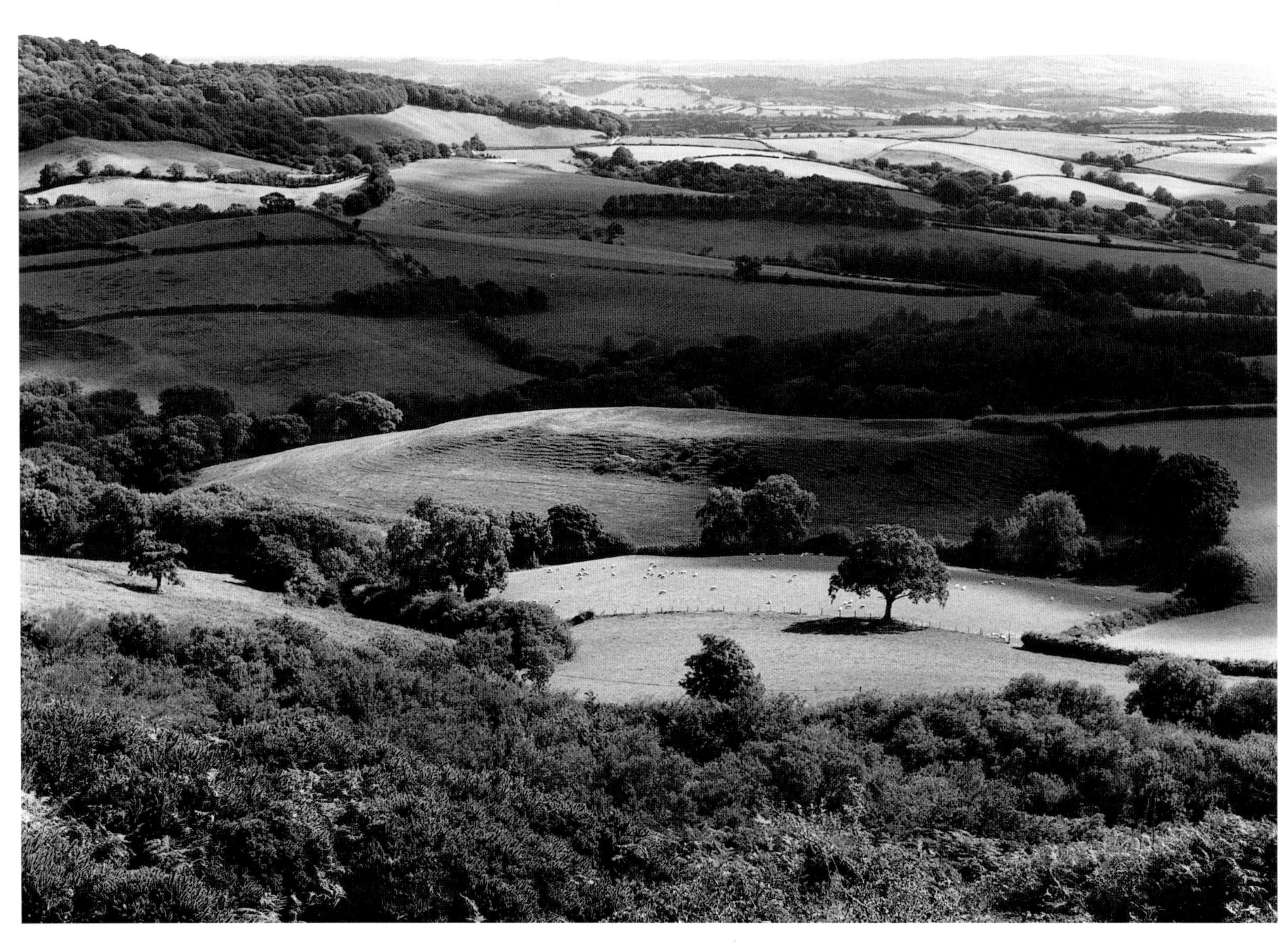

The Marshwood Vale, Lewesdon and Eggardon, from Pilsdon Pen, Dorset by Christopher Rimmer

INTRODUCTION

The West Country is saturated with literary associations, many of which have special meaning to me. Hardy's literary empire stretches the length and breadth of five counties, from Wiltshire in the north to Cornwall, termed 'Farthest Wessex', in the south. I was born in a gamekeeper's cottage on the western edge of the Marshwood Vale, Hardy's Lower Wessex (Devon) and grew up in the shadows of the ancient Dorset hill forts, Pilsdon, Lewesdon and Eggardon.

These great historical landmarks that guard the valleys of the West Country have, for many years, inspired poets, novelists, artists and naturalists. Many of these sites were familiar haunts for the characters from Hardy's novels and, as I grew up, I happily shared his partly real, partly dream country. Often as I meander through this beautiful landscape I find myself engrossed in the visions he created. As I walk in his literary traces, the lasting images of his storytelling invade my mind and suddenly I am transported to another of his chapters or verses, in the shadows of time. On woodland walks, I sometimes imagine what it would be like to meet Giles Winterborne, 'autumn's very brother', at the next woodland clearing.

Dorset still offers the traveller a chance to dream and retreat 'far from the madding crowd', where time stands still and where land is mainly farmed in a more traditional way, resisting some of the harsh, drastic changes of the past century. The tiny patchwork field systems make up this unique Dorset landscape, with hills gently rising and falling away, down to where the land meets the sea.

Paul Harvey's image of the Cobb (plate 10) is home to John Fowles' *The French Lieutenant's Woman*. In this novel, John Fowles introduces us to Sarah, a mysterious creature of the Undercliff in Lyme Regis. Hardyesque in style, it extends the storytelling craft and it has been said to be the first Dorset novel to upstage the work of Thomas Hardy. John Fowles and others have been inspired by the places, faces and traces of other literary figures from the past; Tennyson, Llewelyn Powys, Jane Austen, to name but a few.

Jane Austen spent much time in the West Country and, in 1818, Lyme Regis became something of a literary shrine when *Persuasion* was published. In her novel, her character Louisa Musgrove tumbles down the famous steps on the Cobb, known as 'Granny's Teeth'. Austen describes Lyme as a remarkable town 'whose principal street almost hurrying into the water ... with its neighbouring Charmouth, Golden Cap and Portland created for her the happiest spot ... for sitting in unwearied contemplation'.

The West Country has not only provided a base for my life's work in photography and photographic education, but also enabled me to focus on the aesthetic beauty of the glorious countryside around me, and on the important environmental issues that concern us all. During my lifetime, I have continued to promote the idea that we are merely 'life tenants' of our land. The beautiful landscapes that we try to capture must remain ecologically sound to pass on to future generations. I try to create this awareness as part of my photographic vision. My students quickly recognise that they are living on a fragile earth and their work often reflects a great respect for both the land and its people.

In his insightful, wonderfully evocative poem, *Crabbing*, John Fowles, it seems, reminds us of the greed and stupidity involved in the way we are polluting the sea and the dreadful legacy of this for future generations. He contrasts this with the double standards we employ when we tell our children that crabs die because of their own mindless greed in hunting for bait in our traps. In the case of crabs, it appears, we think that they are partly responsible for their own fate. We do not see the implications here for our own behaviour.

However, we must not lose sight of the positive work that some environmentalists continue to do. In the recent past, the journalist and active environmentalist, Kenneth Allsop, fought long and hard to convince people of the importance of maintaining and sustaining the rich biodiversity of our land. I recall one such campaign on the slopes of Eggardon Hill. Allsop moved from his West London home to live in a disused watermill in the remote Dorset village of West Milton. He campaigned until his death in 1973, focusing our attention on issues involving the threat to wildlife, particularly through the excessive use of pesticides and the destruction of habitats.

Allsop empathised with the natural world. He made us aware that the protection of the countryside should not be left to local councils or even self-appointed conservation bodies. Each person should take responsibility and action, to fight greedy, uninformed exploitation. Allsop became a warrior of his Eggardon hill fort and this was a battle he had to win. He fought off the Forestry Commission's plan to fell acres of primeval oak forest on Powerstock Common, which was to be replanted with conifers. Triumphantly, the forest was handed over to the Dorset Wildlife Trust and currently provides a range of habitats for wildlife. Powerstock Common and the hill fort are home to many precious species, such as the harebell, buzzards, kestrels, skylarks and the adonis blue butterfly.

Christopher Rimmer (plate 16) has captured an evocative image of Marshwood Vale from Pilsdon Pen hill fort looking out across the ancient landscape, showing Lewesdon and Eggardon. The forts dominate the landscape for miles around.

The beautiful curving lines seen in Dianne Dowling's image of Eggardon (plate 6) place the viewer boldly within the bosom of the hill fort. This compression of the landscape accentuates the shape and form of the hill fort, and produces a visually powerful image. These Iron Age hill forts were built by local farming communities around 300-500BC. As we gaze out over this ancient landscape, we dream about the first settlers and how they worked the land. The dominion of wind, cloud and turf evokes strong feelings of an ancient bygone age.

In its literary traces, Eggardon is the Norcombe Hill of Hardy's *Far from the Madding Crowd*: 'Norcombe Hill, not far from lonely Toller-Down; one of the spots which suggest to a passer-by that he is in the presence of a shape approaching the indestructible as nearly as any to be found on earth'. Moving in a westerly direction from Eggardon, we may stumble upon the small rural village of Pymore on the River Brit. Pymore was a complete Victorian working village and a thriving rope-making industry existed here; the old factory survives to be remembered as a fine example of an industrial development in harmony with nature and one that should be emulated.

The River Brit runs down into Bridport, Hardy's Port Bredy, then down into West Bay. The vertical sea-cliffs here are ideal habitats for fulmars and gulls. This dramatic coastline has been captured by Ulick Palmer (plate 88) in his spectacular image of West Bay from Thorncombe Beacon. These stunning views can be experienced all along the coastal path down to Lyme Regis and on into Devon.

The Axe Estuary in Devon is home to many birds. The most commonly seen are the redshank, a wading bird with bright red legs now localised in South West England. Another breed to be found in the Axe is the little egret, which looks like a small white heron, that up until ten years ago, was rare in the UK. And of course there is the kingfisher, with its radiant bright blue and orange colours which is found in lowland rivers and can be spotted right down to the sea. Keith Smith (plate 83) has produced a moody riverbank scene of the River Axe. We often see the river in the mist but it is rarely captured in such an evocative way.

For some years now, I have organised and lectured on many photographic courses. The topics cover landscapes, nature, people in the environment, and architecture. During my courses and summer schools, I included location photography on the Somerset Levels.

Some 5000 years ago, the Levels were covered by sea and now are characterised by reeds, willow trees and slow-flowing rivers. Pollarding, a form of tree management, has been practised on the Somerset Levels since the Bronze Age. This unique area, noted for its basket- and hurdle-making, is where arrowhead, cotton grass and marsh marigold still flourish. Richard Bland's image of cows grazing by a rhyne at West Sedgemoor (plate 26) captures the character of this unique wetland. The Somerset rivers, wandering indolently across the plains, are all tributaries of the Severn. The rivers that flow down through the Levels - the Brue, the Cary, the Parrett and the Tone - find that their paths are virtually blocked. The Levels are formed in part by the surge of sea-floods coming in from the Bristol Channel and by the floods from the rain on the surrounding hills.

Tall willow wands are planted in beds on the moors and cut to ground level in winter. By autumn again, the following year, they have grown eight feet high. It is quite magical to think that a withy can grow three inches on a hot, sunny day. From a full summer sprouting of growth to a contrasting winter flatness, this carefully managed landscape of meadow and water has been controlled by the local residents for many years. All this forms part of the character of the Levels. Water under control is the life of the place.

As we return to Dorset, one of my much-visited sites is Whitchurch Canonicorum. It is said to be the 'capital' of the Marshwood Vale, yet most people may never discover this charming, out-of-the-way village, apart from the genuine traveller such as Justin Orwin's *Pilgrim* (plate 36). The church not only offers a quiet, meditative resting place, but also a wealth of history and architectural beauty. The church has many Norman features and is dedicated to both St. Cross, and St. Candida, whose shrine is placed in the north transept. This beautiful architecture is typical of the many ancient churches in the West Country. Denise Owen's contribution (plate 37) gives us some insight into this wonderful church at Whitchurch Canonicorum.

As we travel further into the Purbeck hills, Corfe Castle stands alone in the unspoilt English countryside. The castle has been captured on canvas by artists such as Paul Nash and more recently by many photographers.

Some architectural images have been chosen particularly for their aesthetic beauty as well as their history. For example, the subject of Rob Dyson's cover image, *Clavel's Tower*, above Kimmeridge Bay, in the Isle of Purbeck, was described by Nicholas Pevsner as 'a scholarly mixture of motifs, as befits a folly: round the bottom, a colonnade of Tuscan columns of the primitive type favoured by French painters, such as David, for their backgrounds, and round the top false machicoulis and a parapet pierced with quatrefoils'. P.D. James used the folly as a frame of reference for her novel *The Black Tower*. Despite her own inventions of architectural sites in the novel, Clavel's Tower is an obvious reference that she refaces in a dark and mysterious way, to set the tone for her crime thriller.

The images I have selected for *Shadows in Time* reveal that our photographers are in tune with nature as well as demonstrating great artistic ability. The fine monochrome prints presented show the clear vision and printing skills needed to produce works of value and artistic merit. They not only create a sense of place, but offer a series of visual stories set in some of this country's most beautiful landscapes. Some of the places here are steeped in history, and others have stories that are lodged deep in the folk memories of successive generations.

Many of the black and white images shown in this collection will hopefully fire your imagination. Maybe they will tempt you into following the literary traces of some of our great writers. The collection forms a unique and exciting body of work, which I hope will bring you long-lasting pleasure.

Ron Frampton

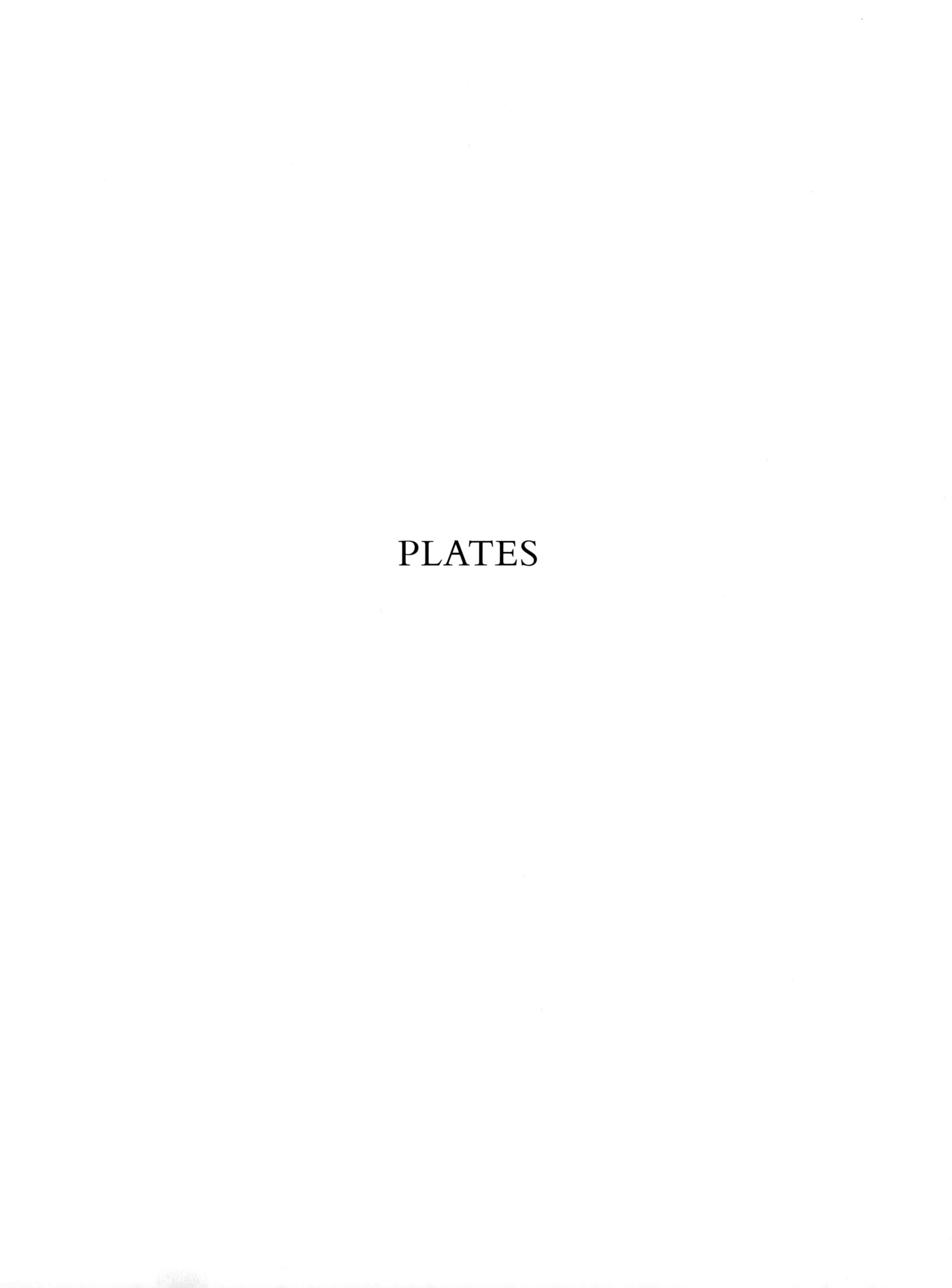

PLATES

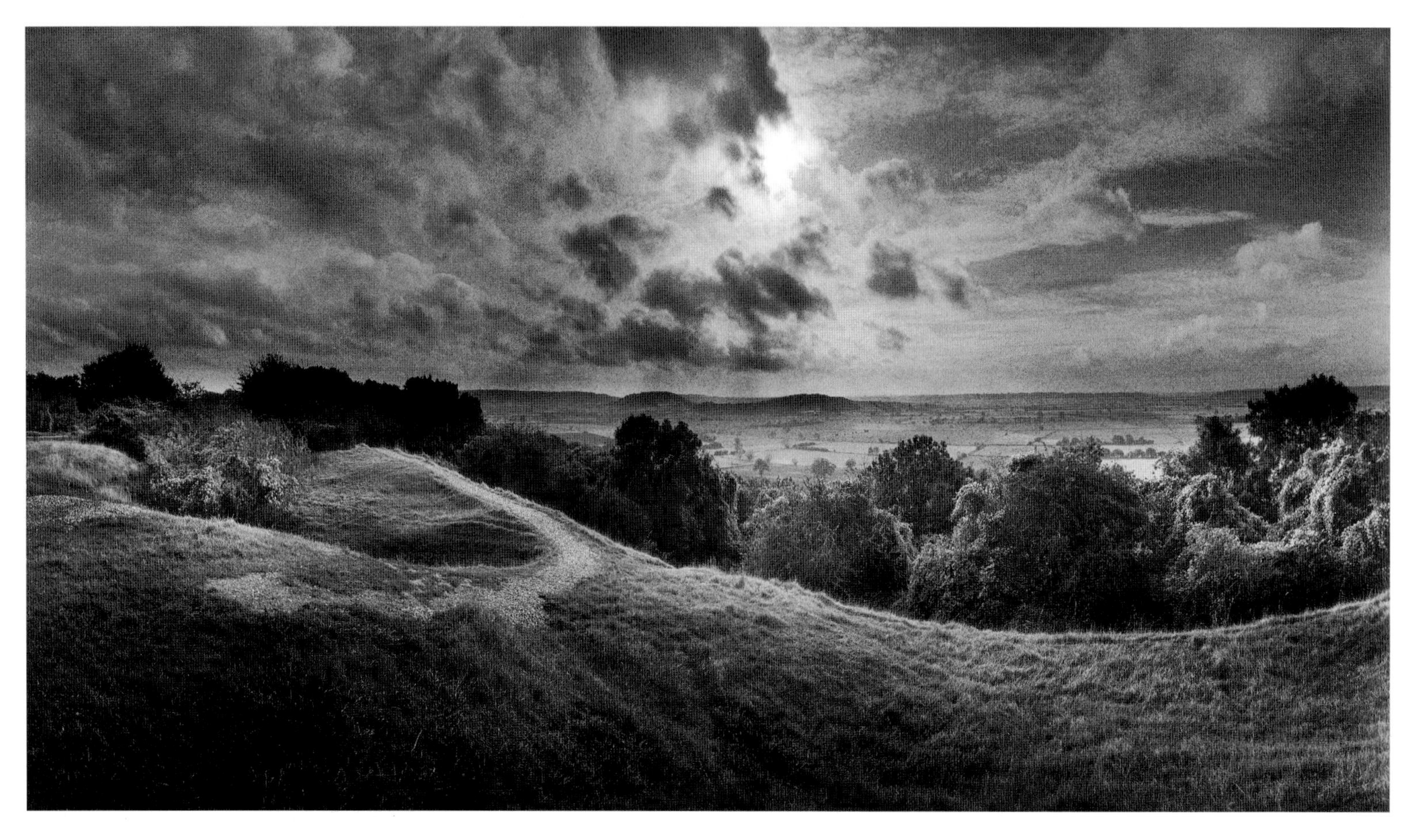

The Somerset Levels, from the Polden Hills, Somerset by Richard Lane

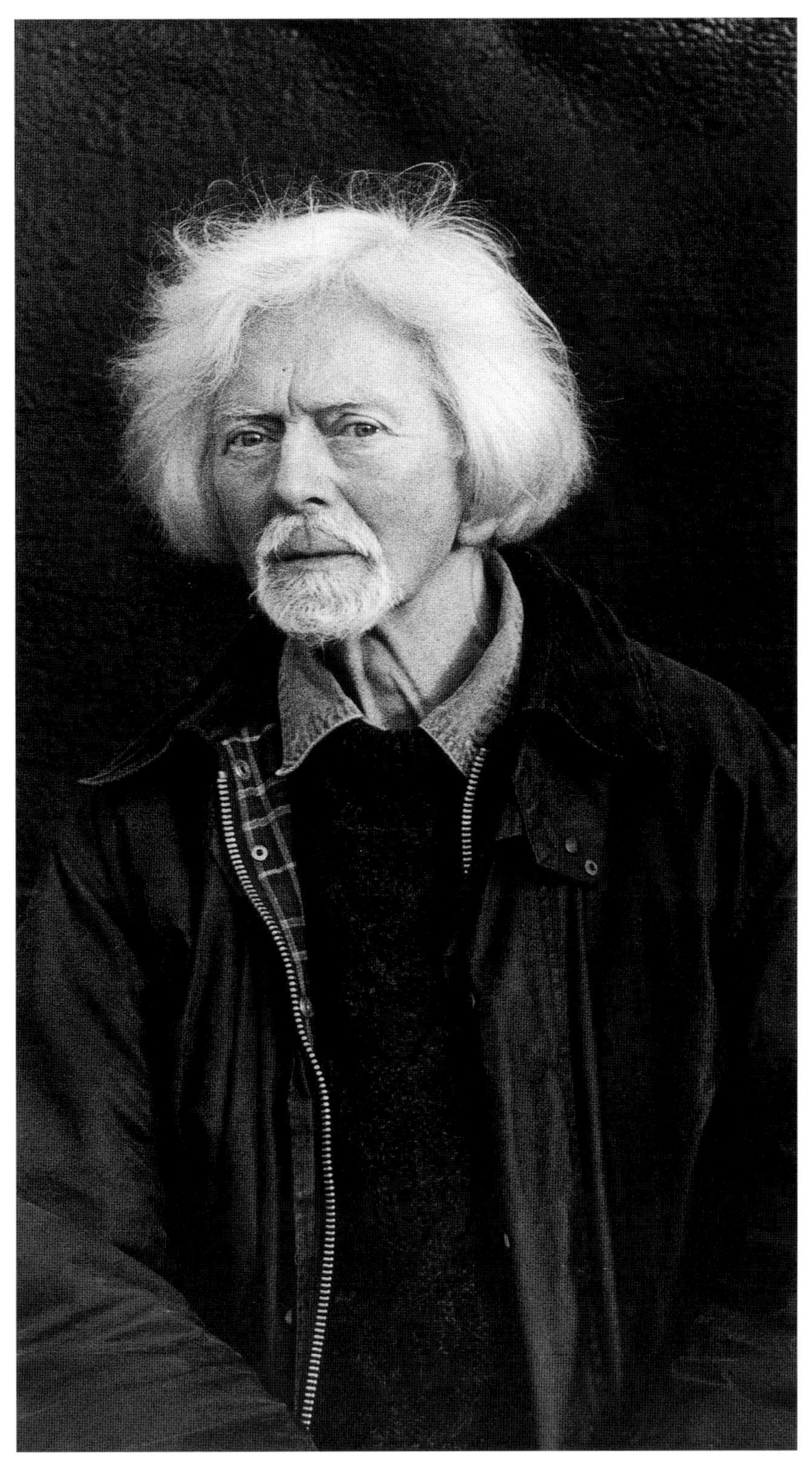

Alan Martin, Storyteller, Hawkchurch, Devon by Katia Marsh

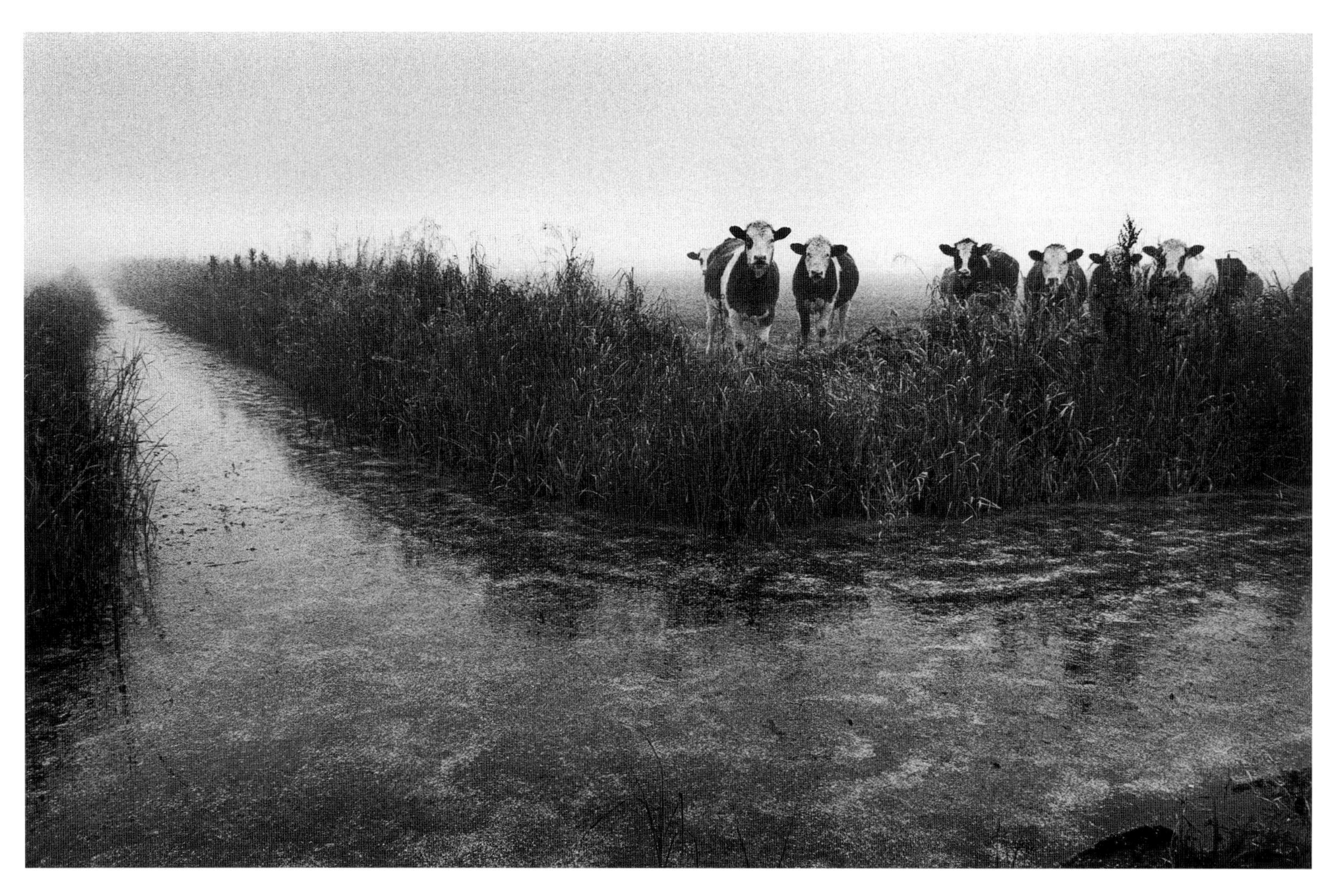

Cattle, West Sedgemoor, Somerset Levels, Somerset by Richard Bland

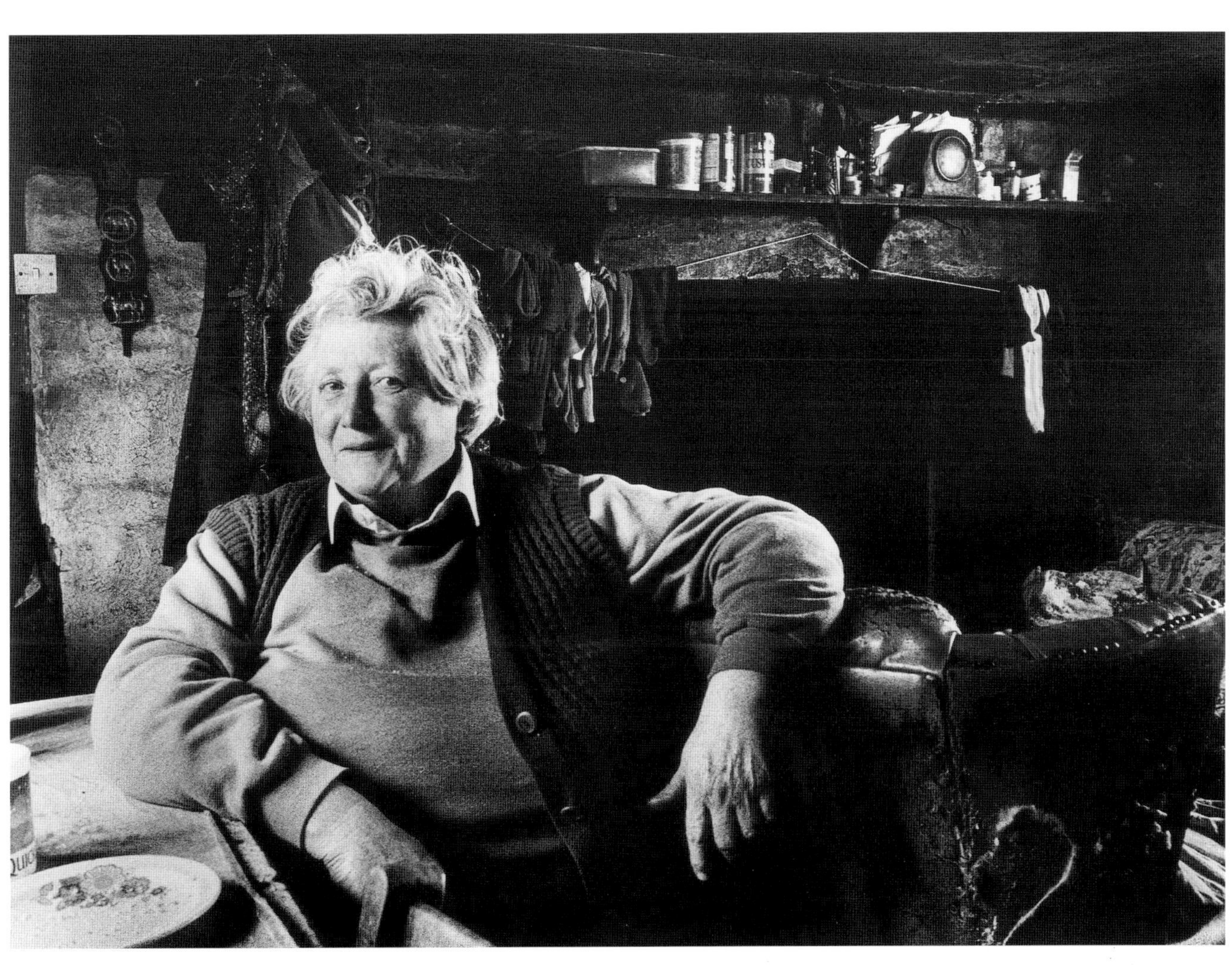

Joan Norris, Farmer, Low Ham, Somerset Levels, Somerset by Pauline Rook

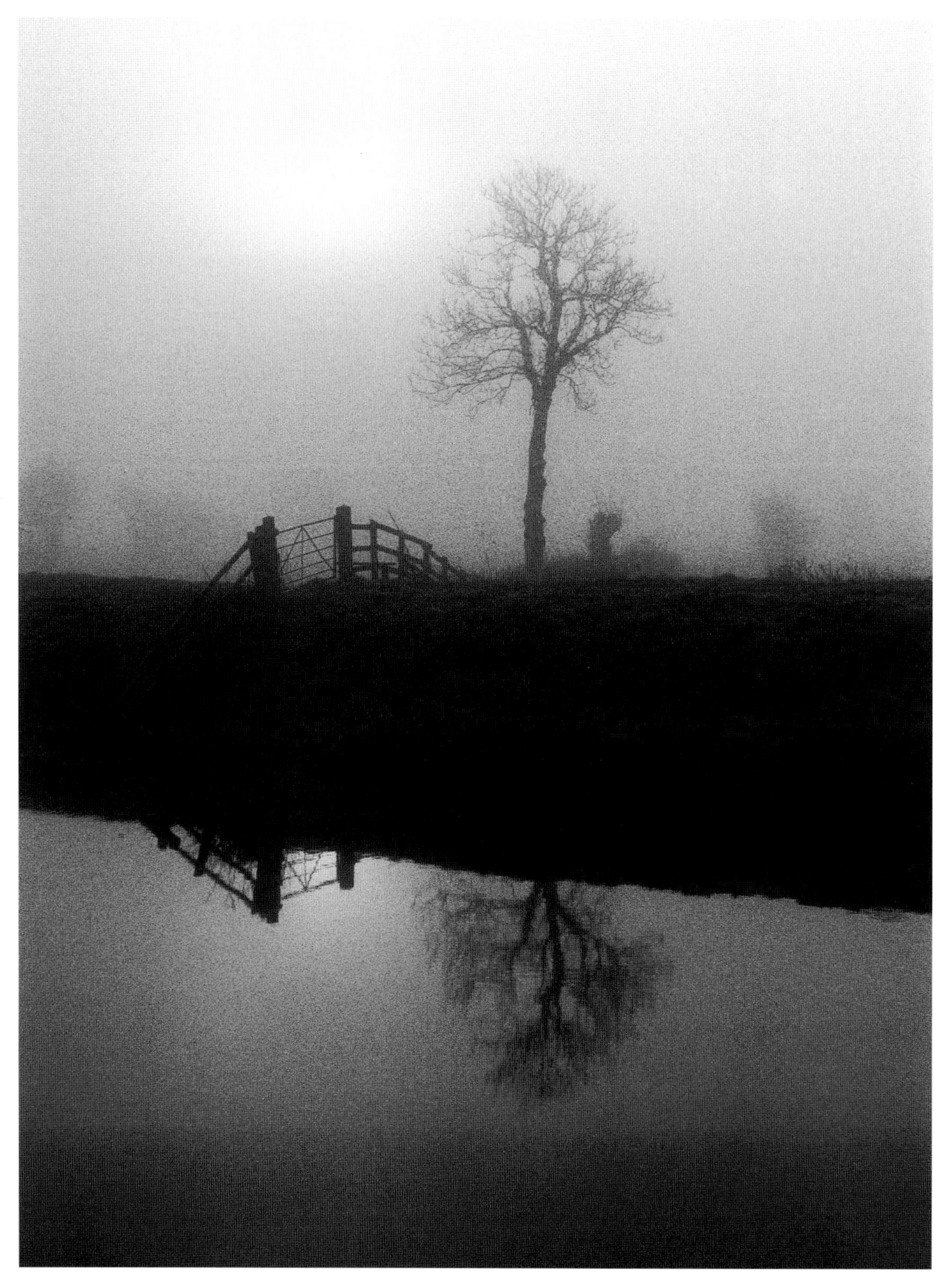

Curry Moor, Somerset Levels, Somerset by Ian Beech

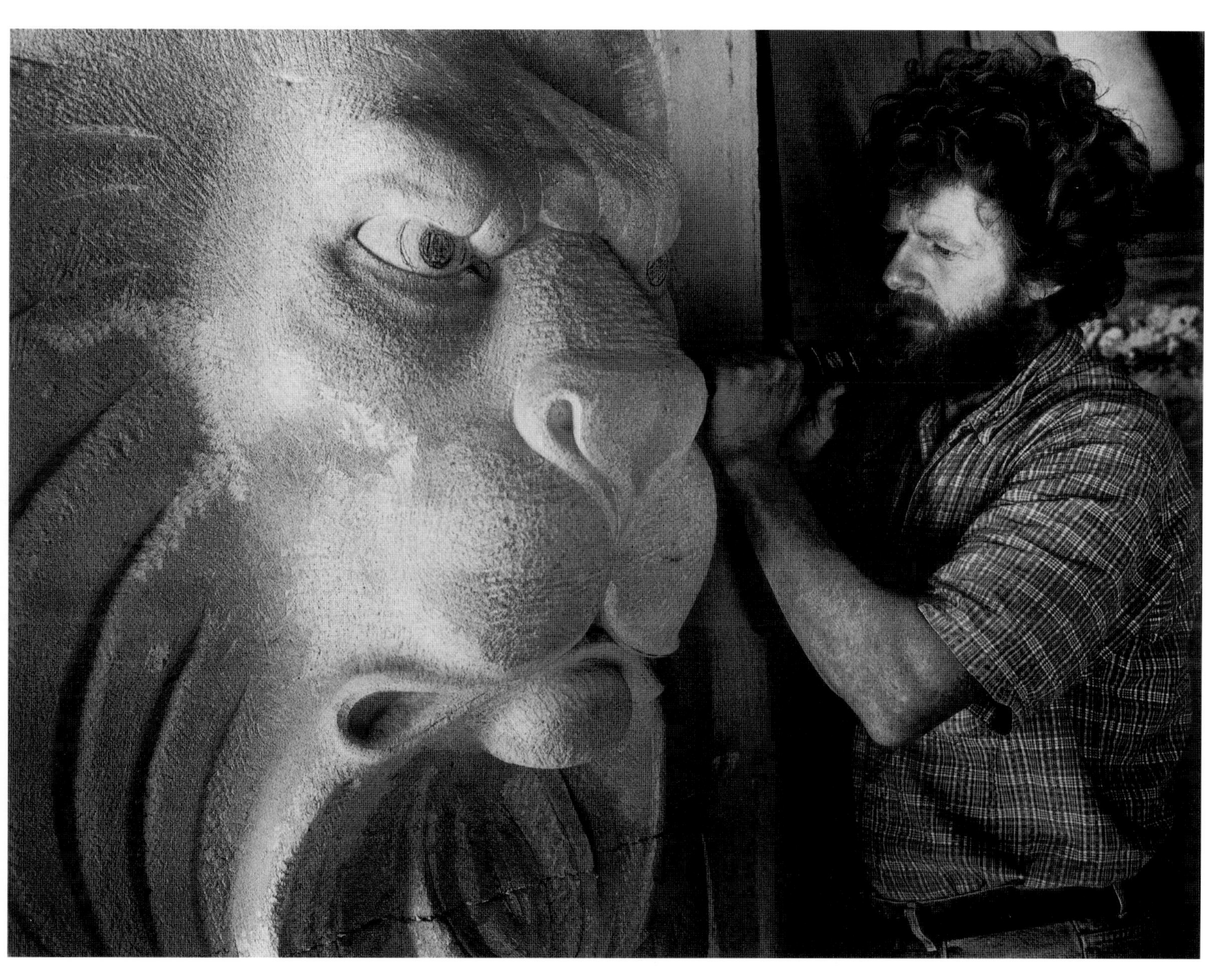

Tom Clarke, Stone-Carver, Martock, Somerset by Justin Orwin

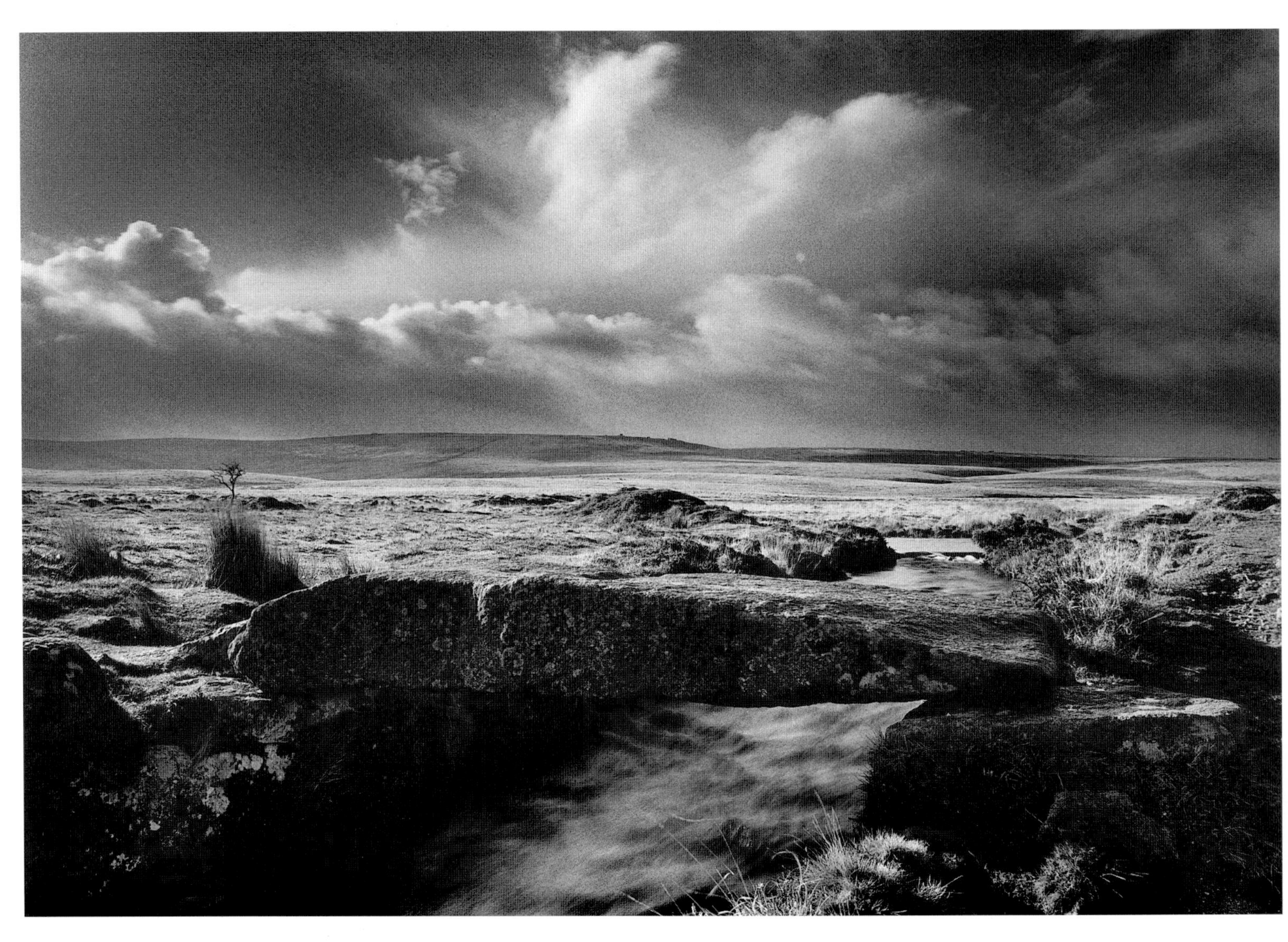

Clapper Bridge, Gidleigh, Dartmoor, Devon by Bob Williams

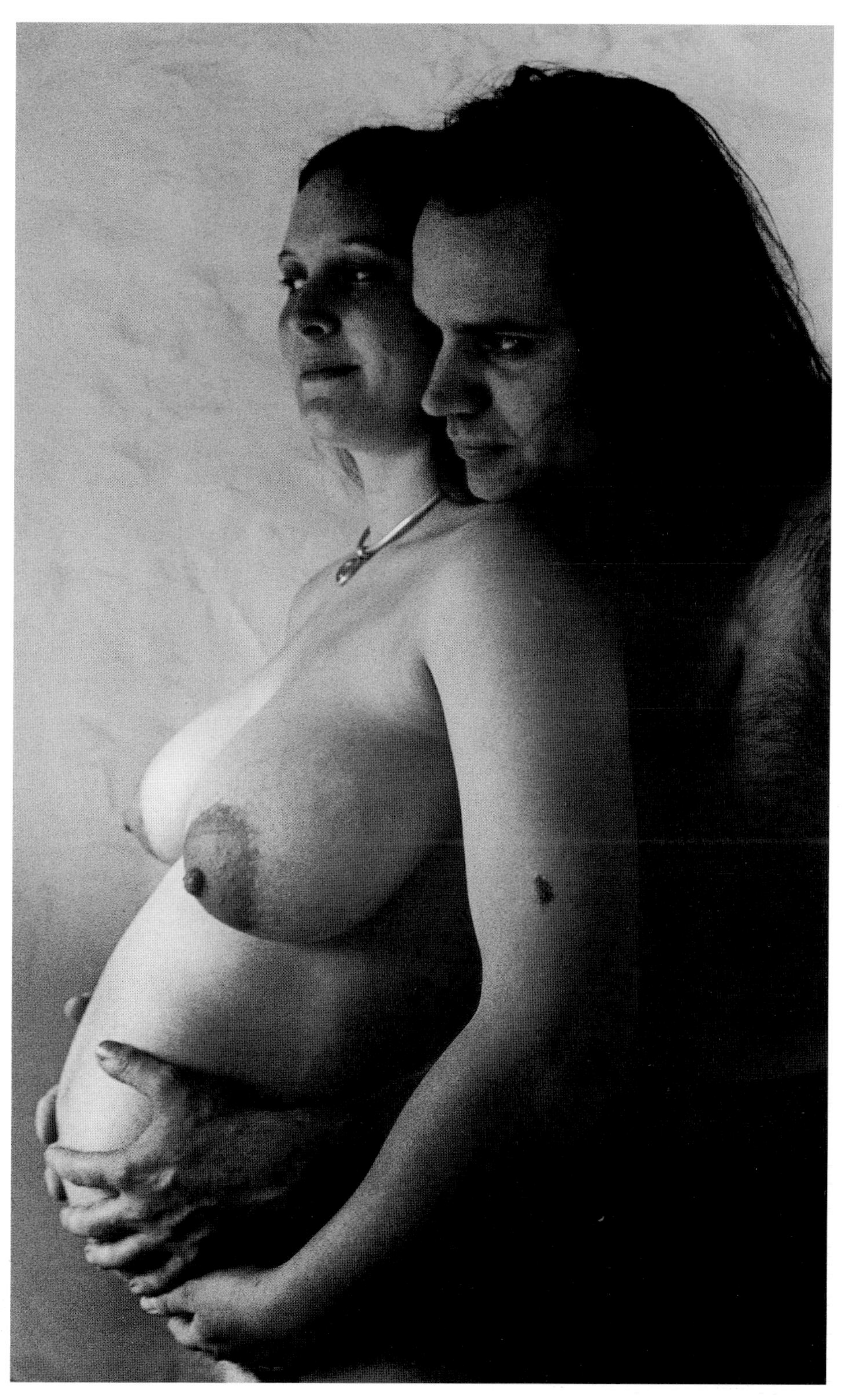

'Awaiting', Yarde, Devon by Dianne Dowling

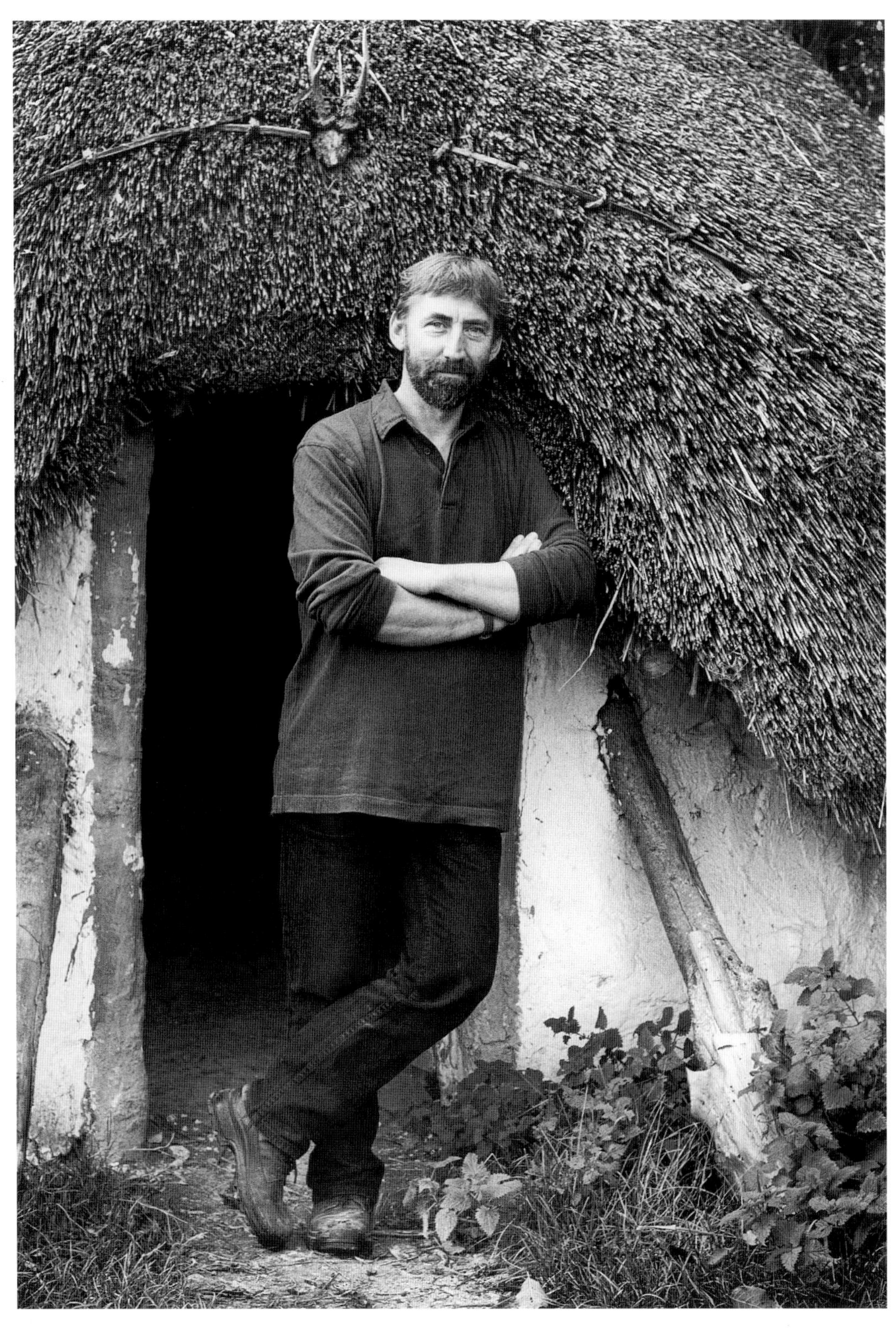

Russel Sydenham and Iron-Age Thatched Hut, Dorset by Robin Mills

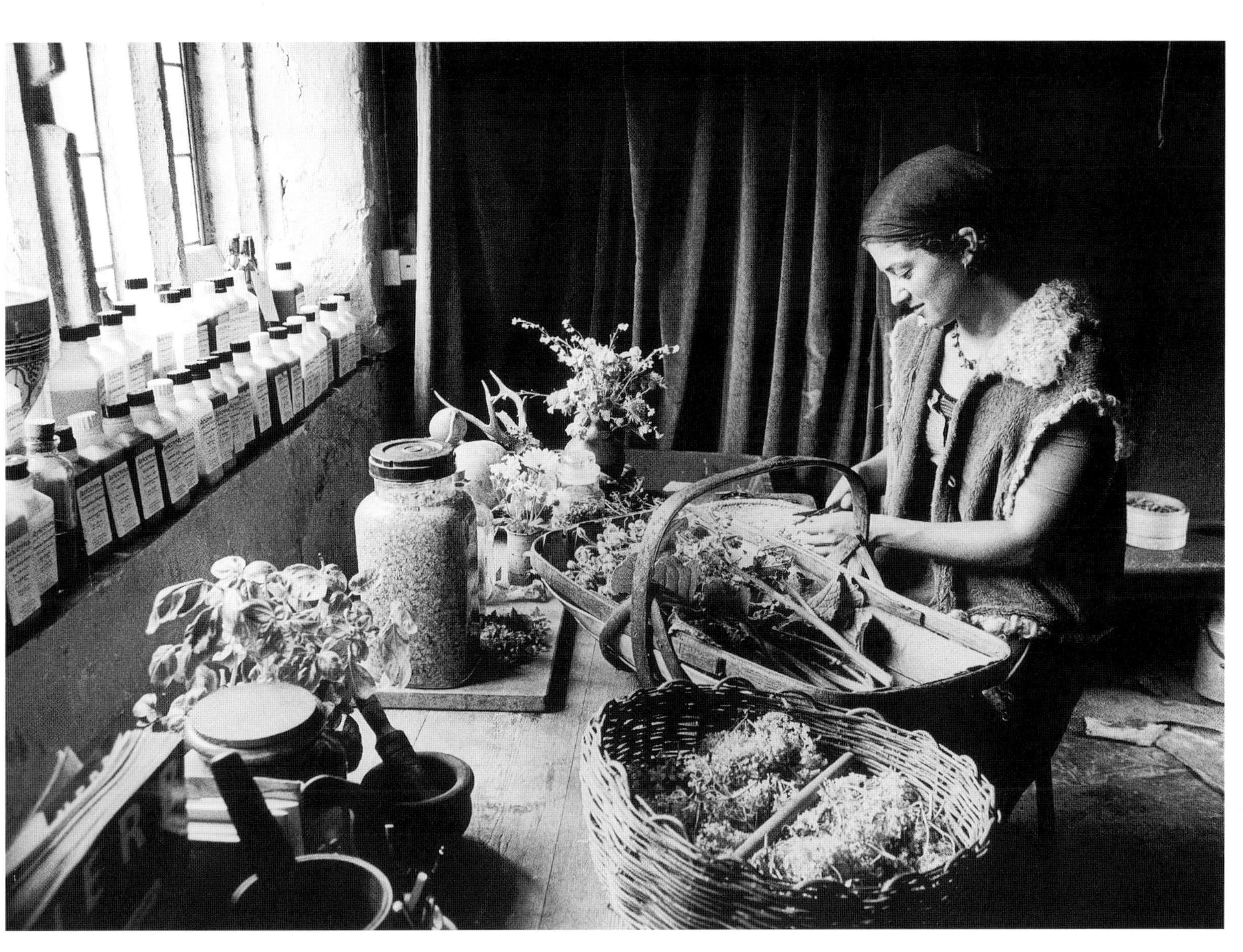

Eleanor Gallia, Medical Herbalist, Dorset by Robin Mills

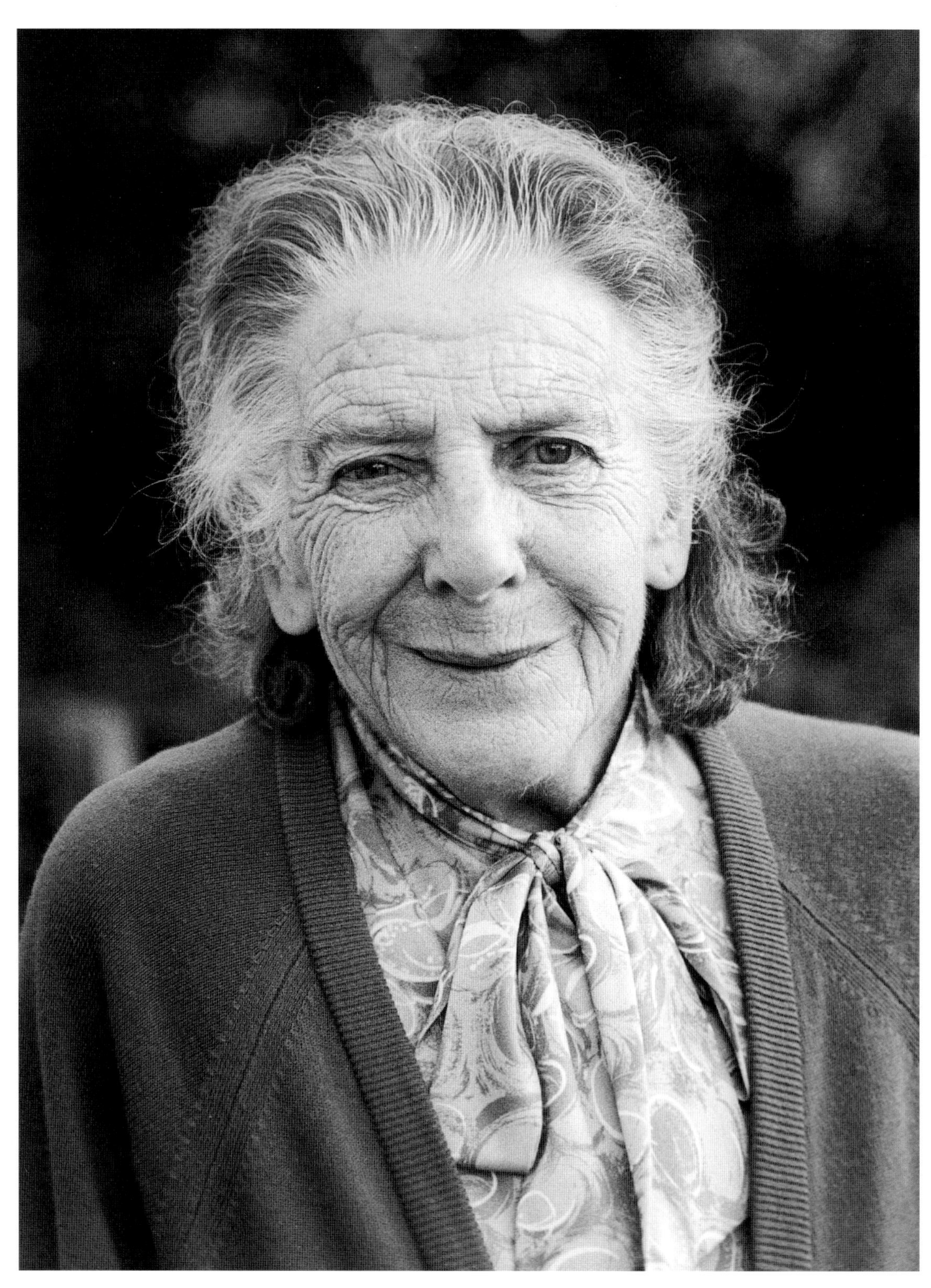

Iris Manning, South Petherton, Somerset by John Nicholson

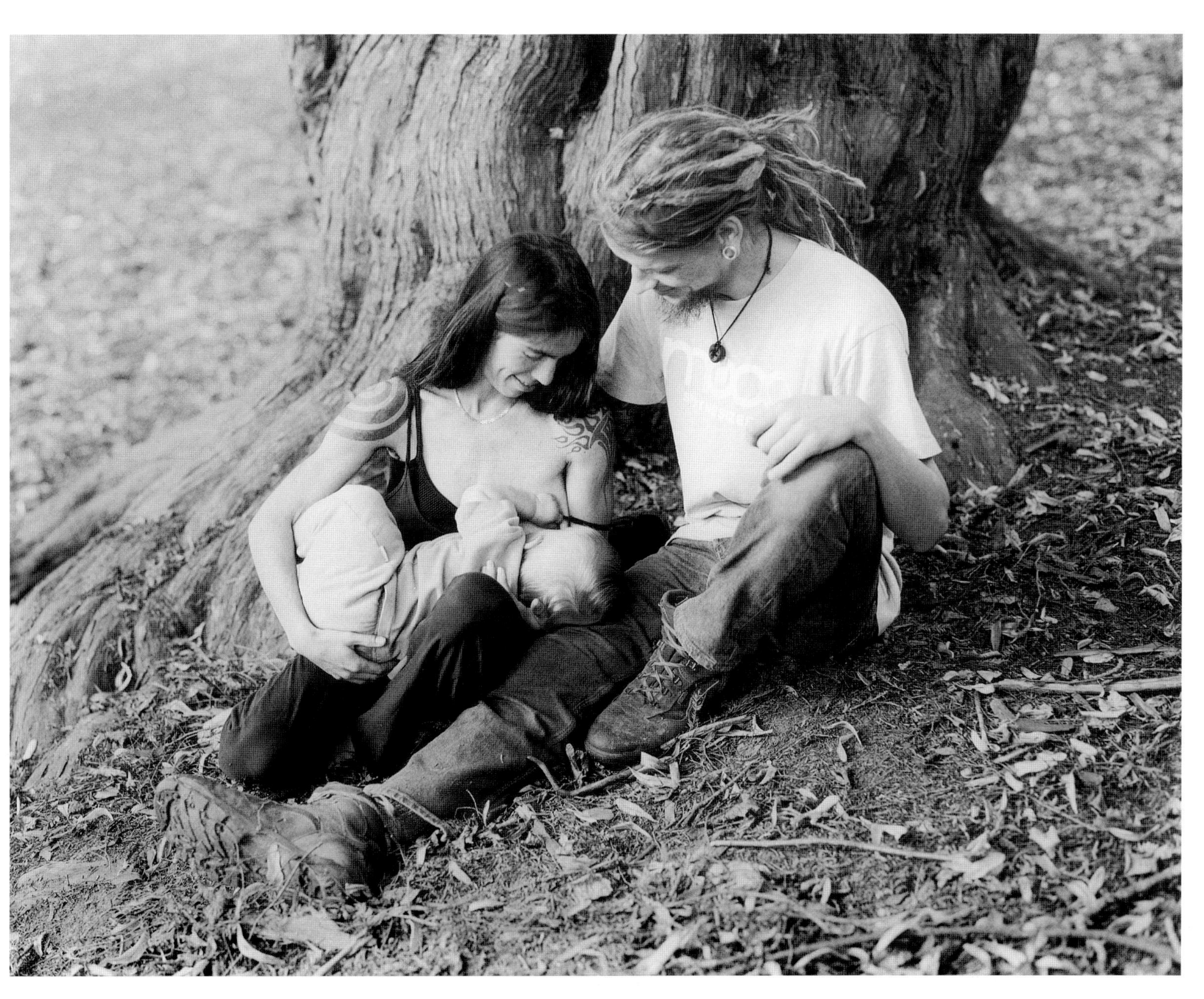

Michael, Kate and Mike, Dillington Woodland, Somerset by Ulick Palmer

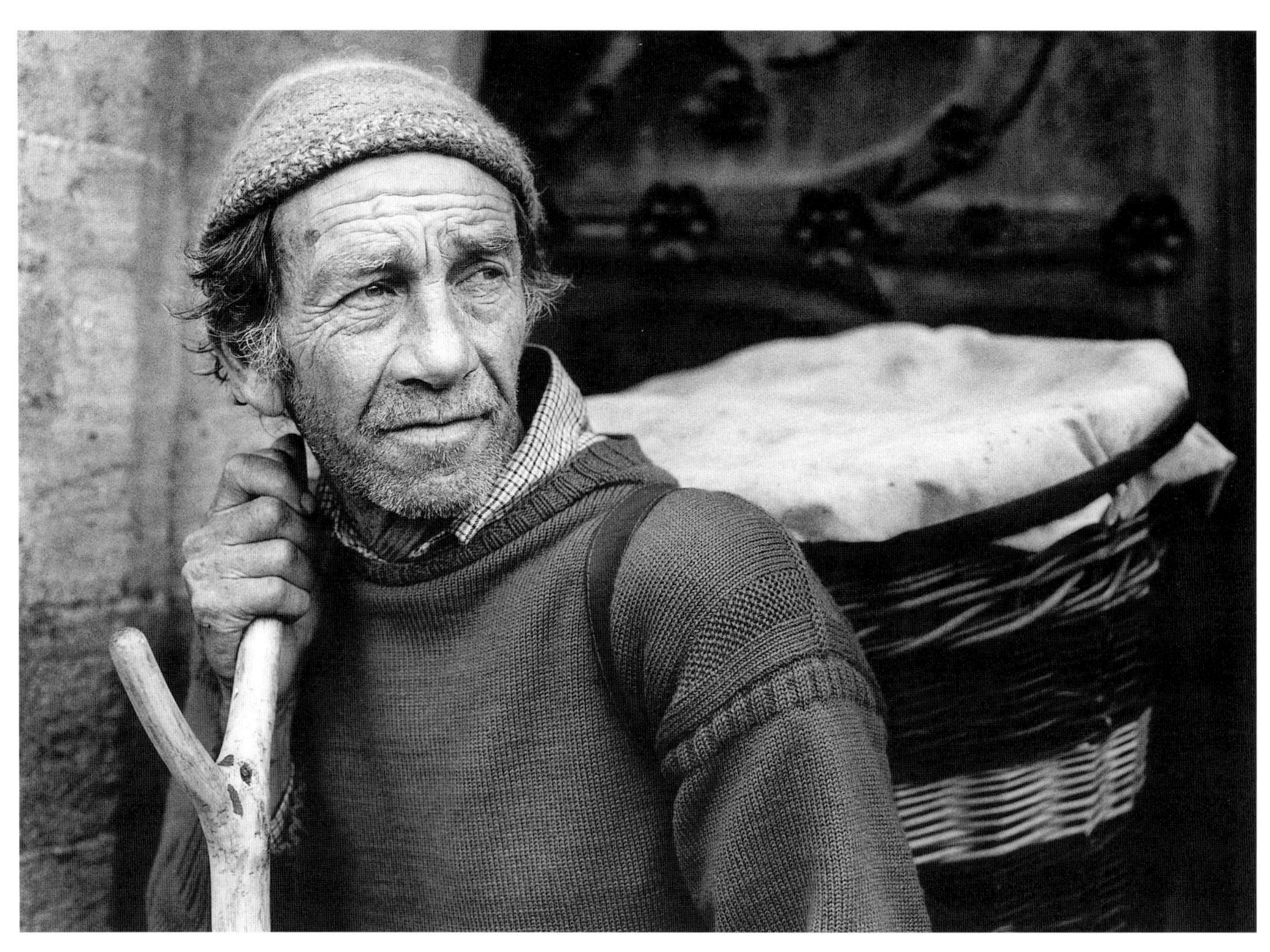

Pilgrim, Somerset by Justin Orwin

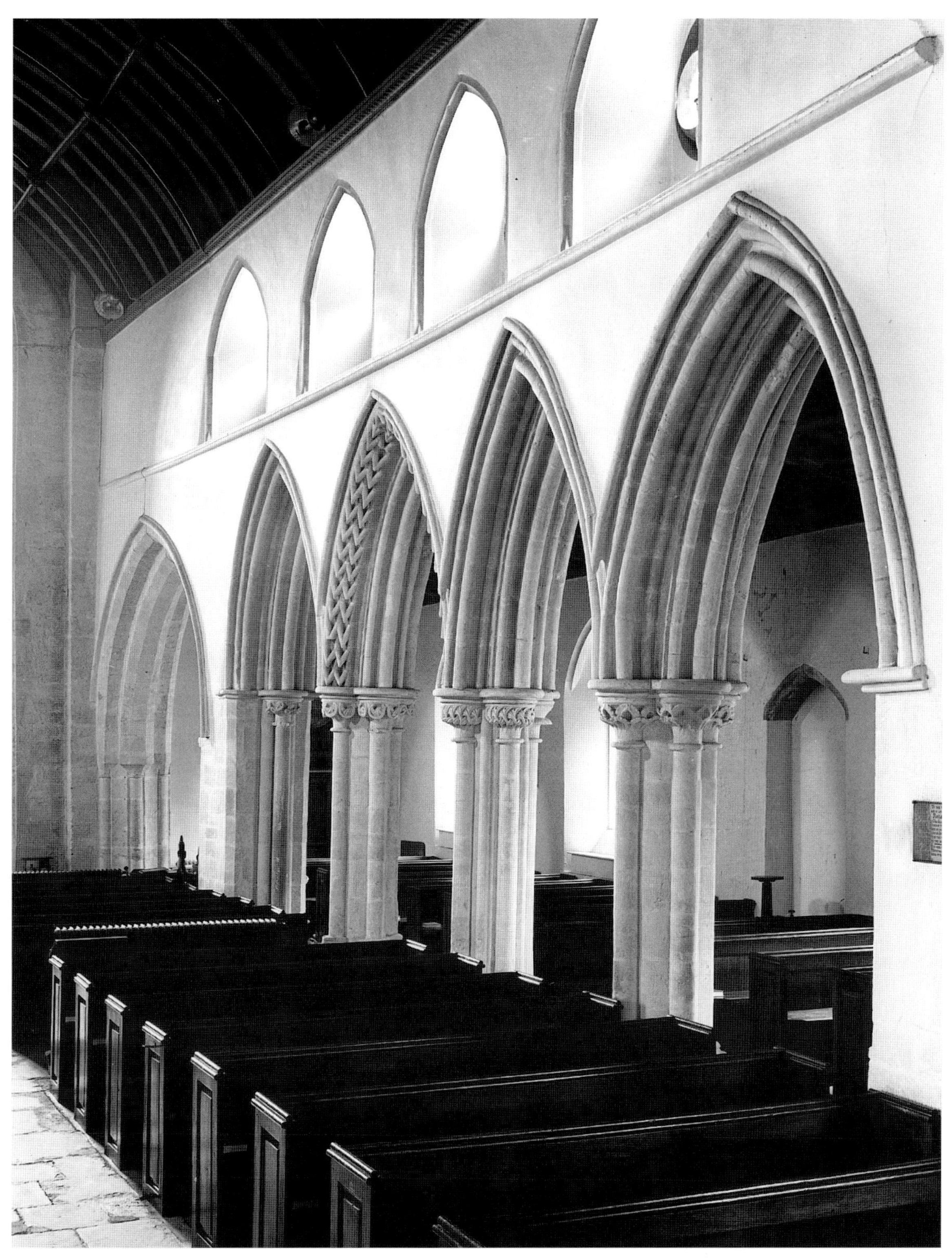

Norman Columns, Whitchurch Canonicorum, Dorset by Denise Owen

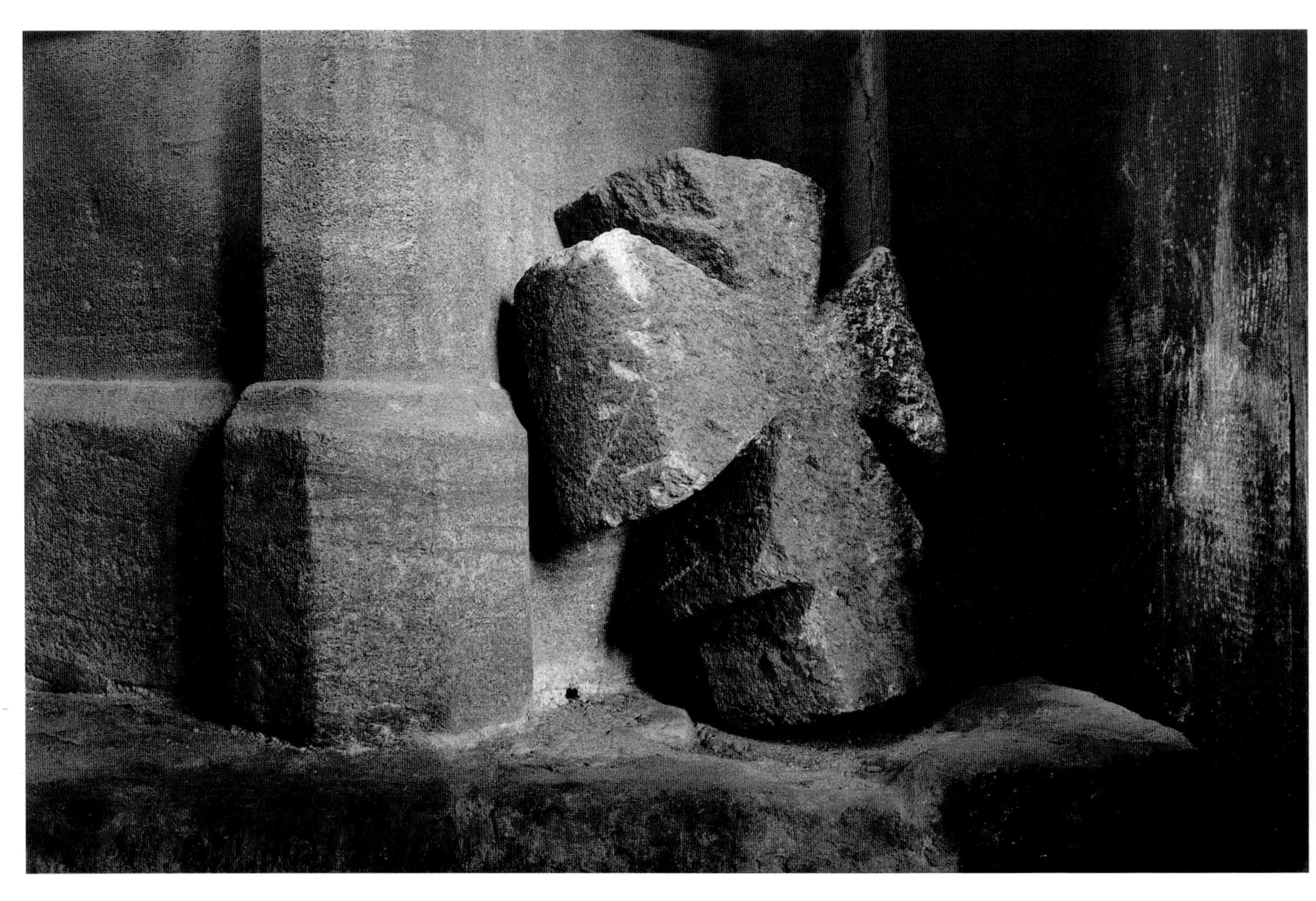

Broken Cross, St. Mary the Virgin, Stocklinch Ottersey, Somerset by Paul Harvey

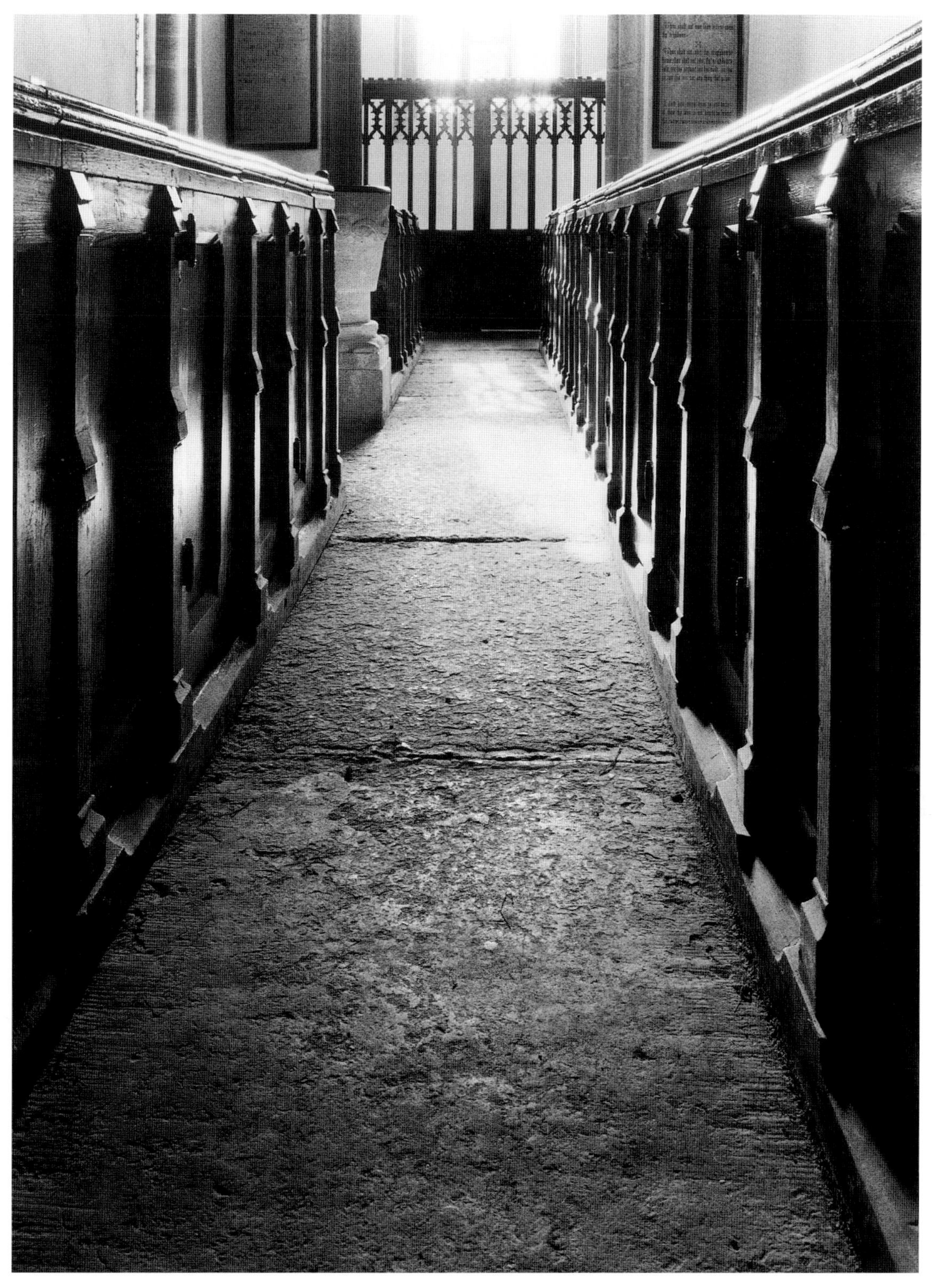

Aisle, St. Mary the Virgin, Stocklinch Ottersey, Somerset by Paul Harvey

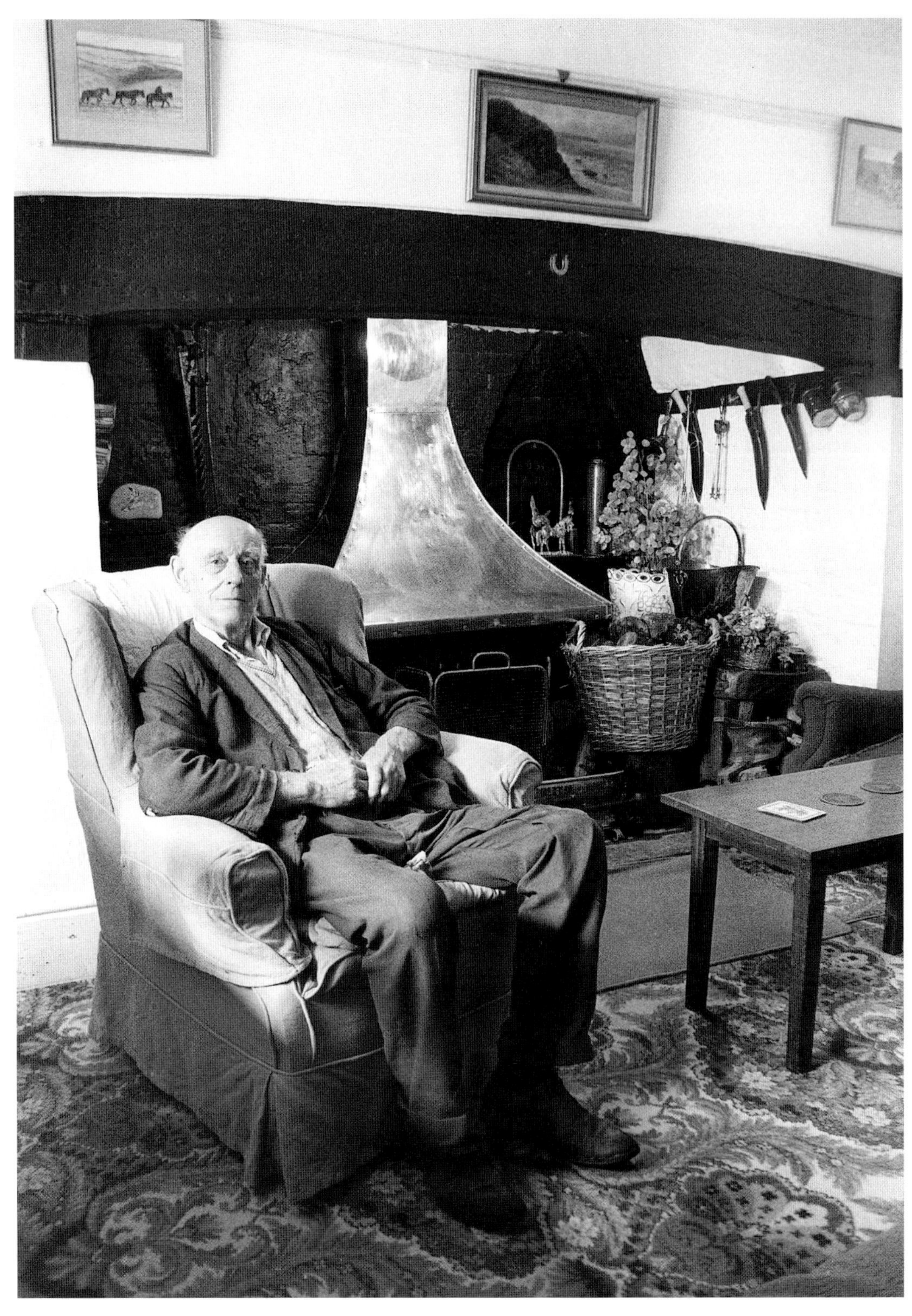

Donald Wyatt sitting by his fireplace, Cudworth, Somerset by Nicky Saunter

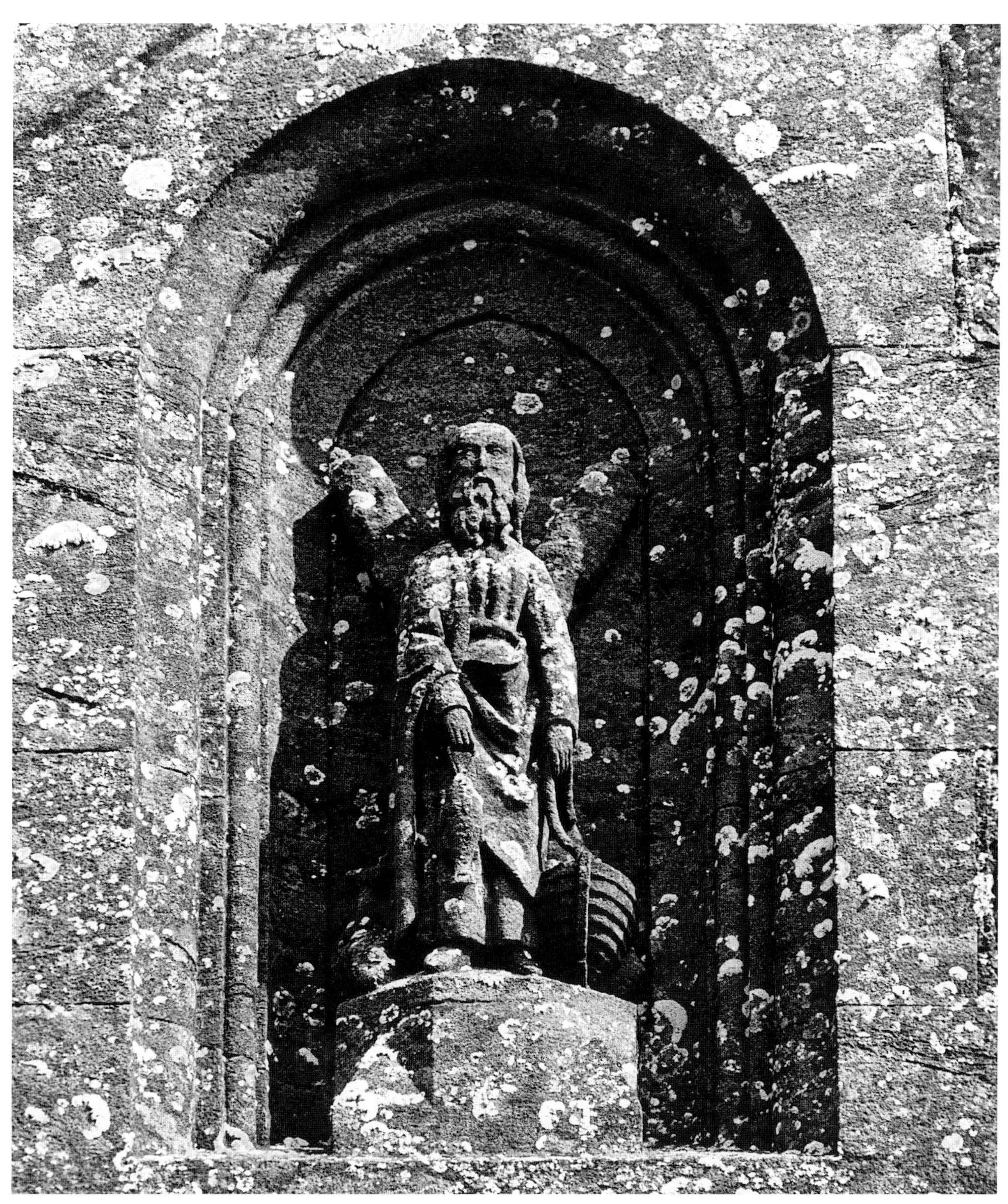

Stone Carving, St. Andrew, Dowlish Wake, Somerset by Sue Milverton

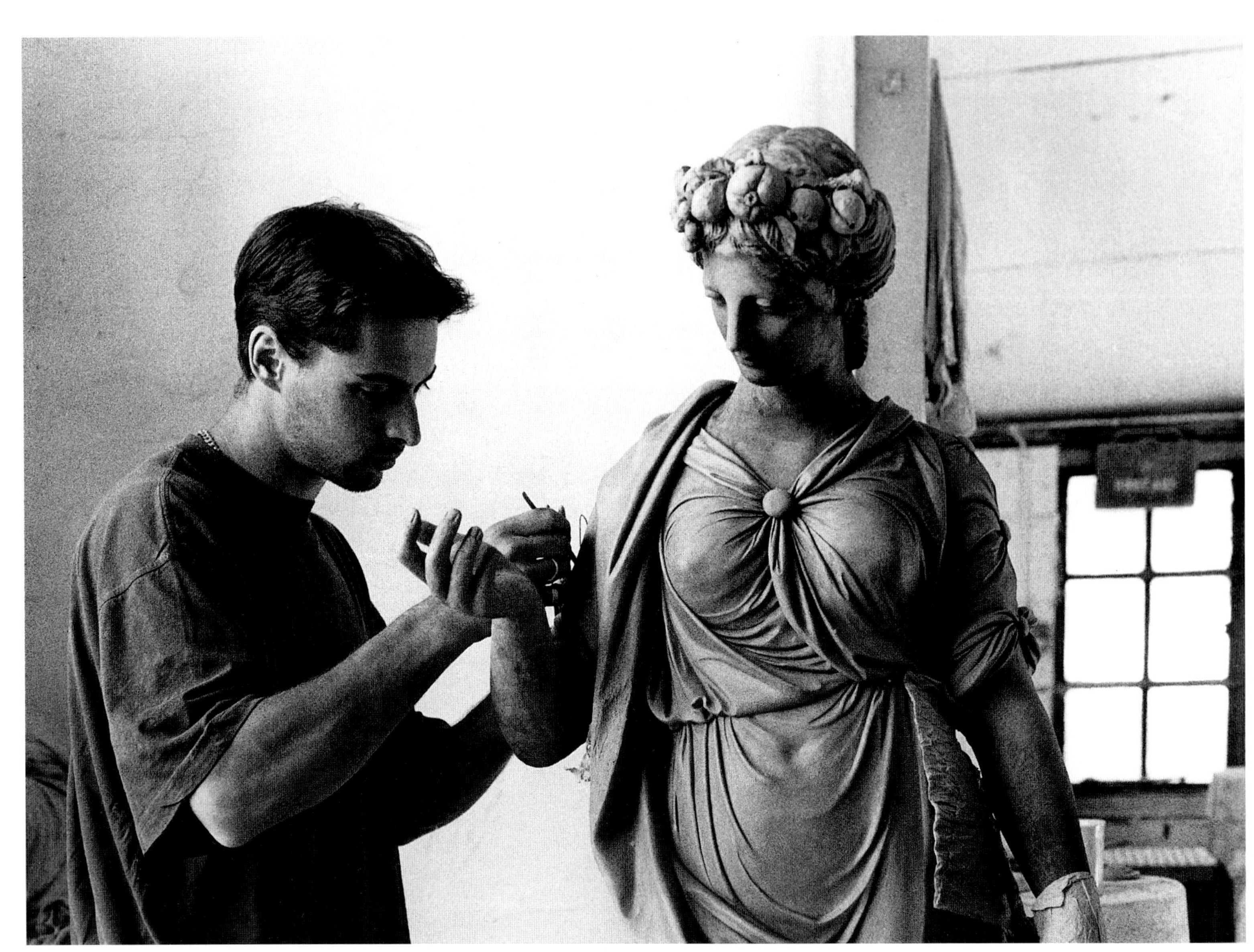

Statue of Pomona by Thomason, Cudworth, Somerset, with Dan Anderson carrying out detail finishing by Nicky Saunter

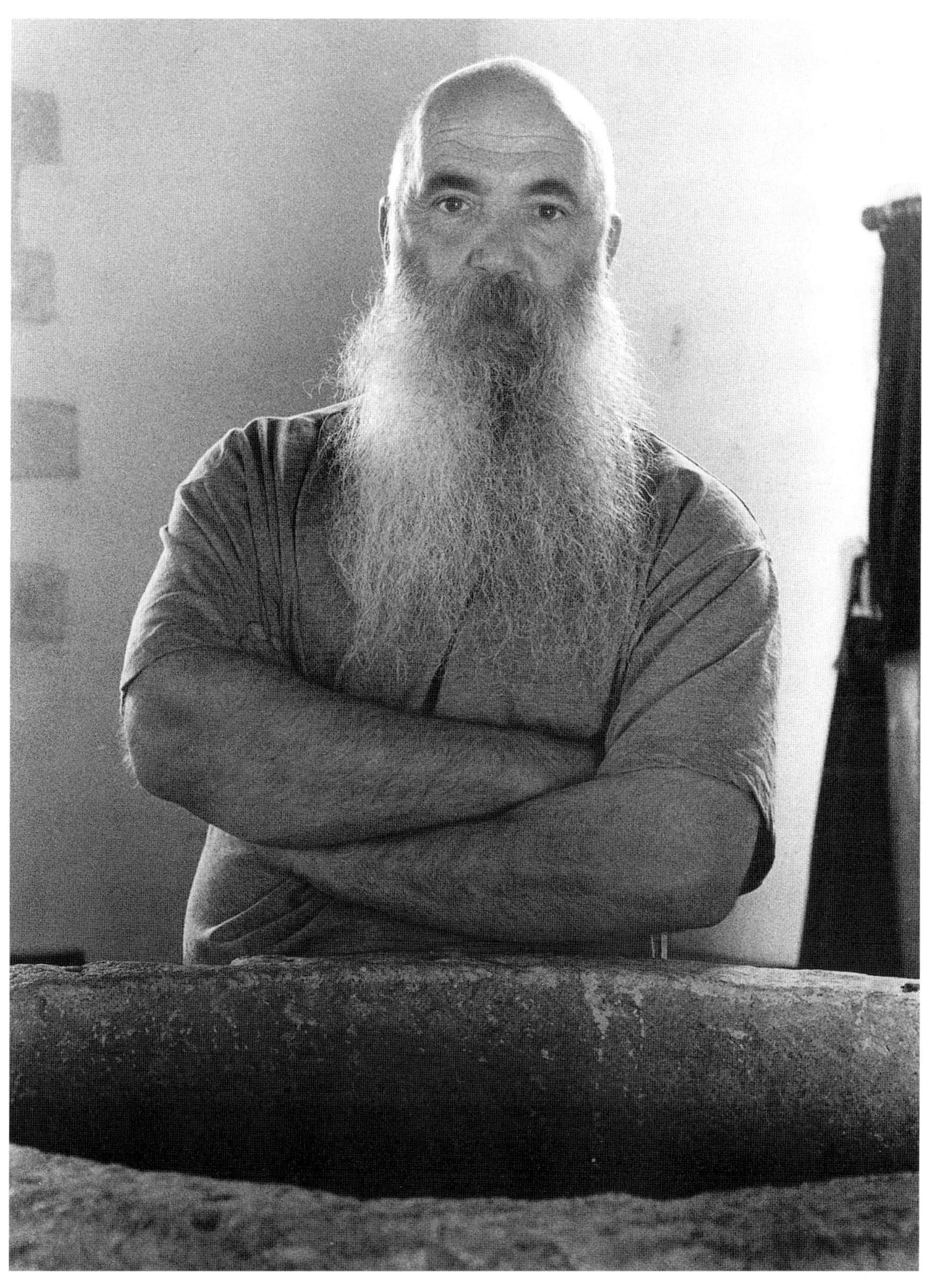

Philip Thomason, Cudworth, Somerset, by Nicky Saunter

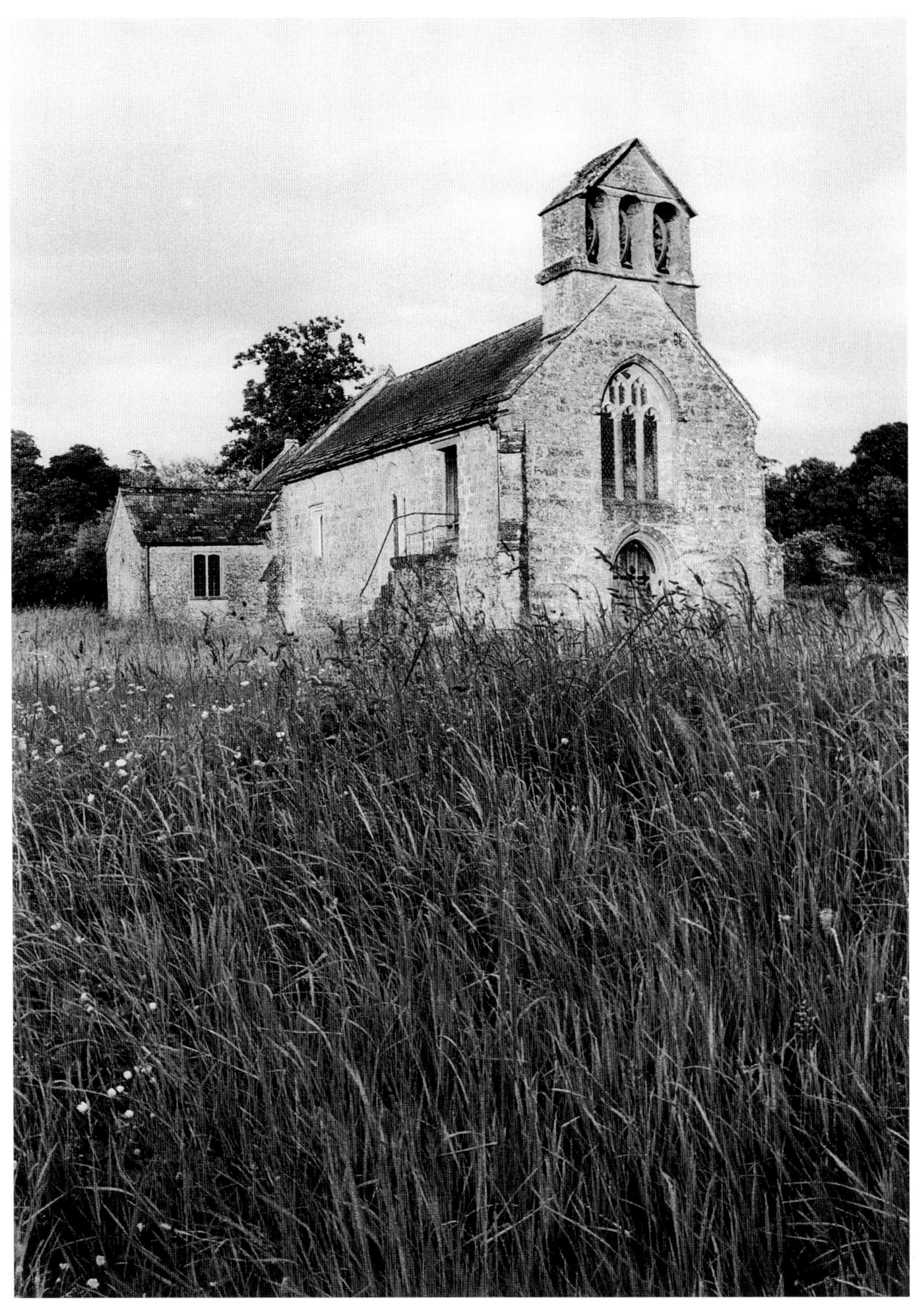

St. Mary Magdalene, Stocklinch, Somerset by Paul Harvey

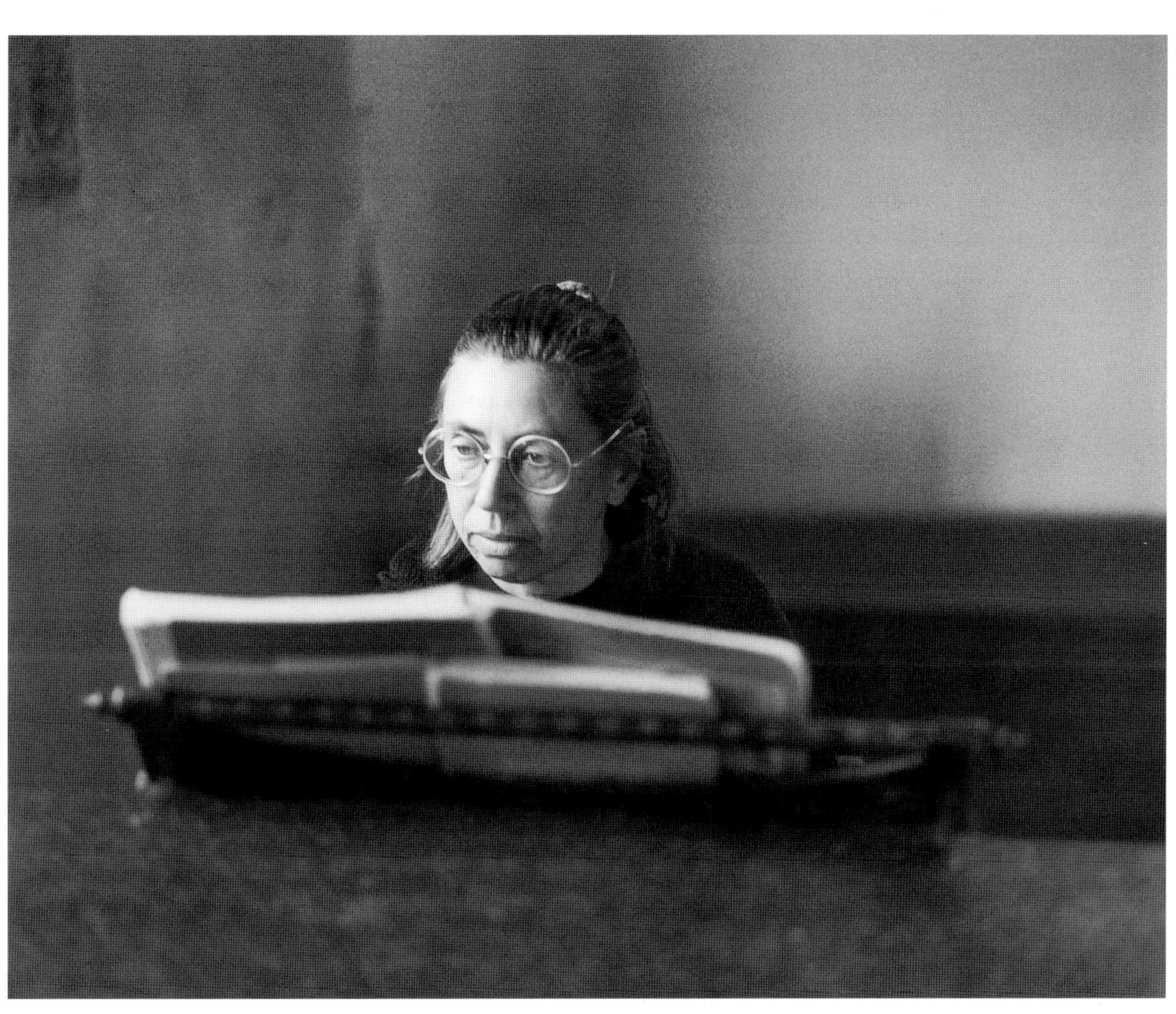

Annemiecke Wigmore, Organist, St. Michael, Cudworth, Somerset by Ulick Palmer

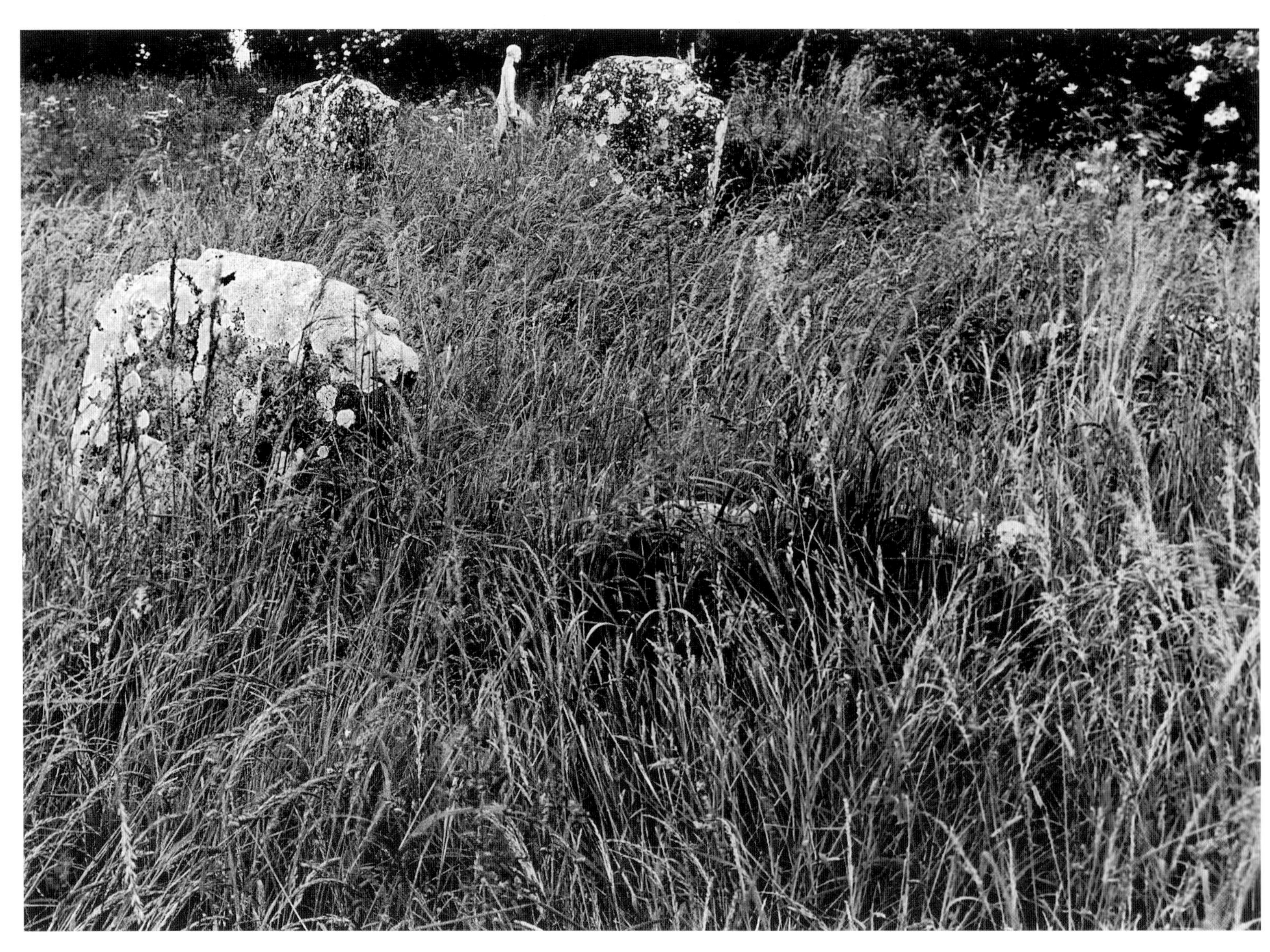

Churchyard, St. James, Chillington, Somerset by Sue Milverton

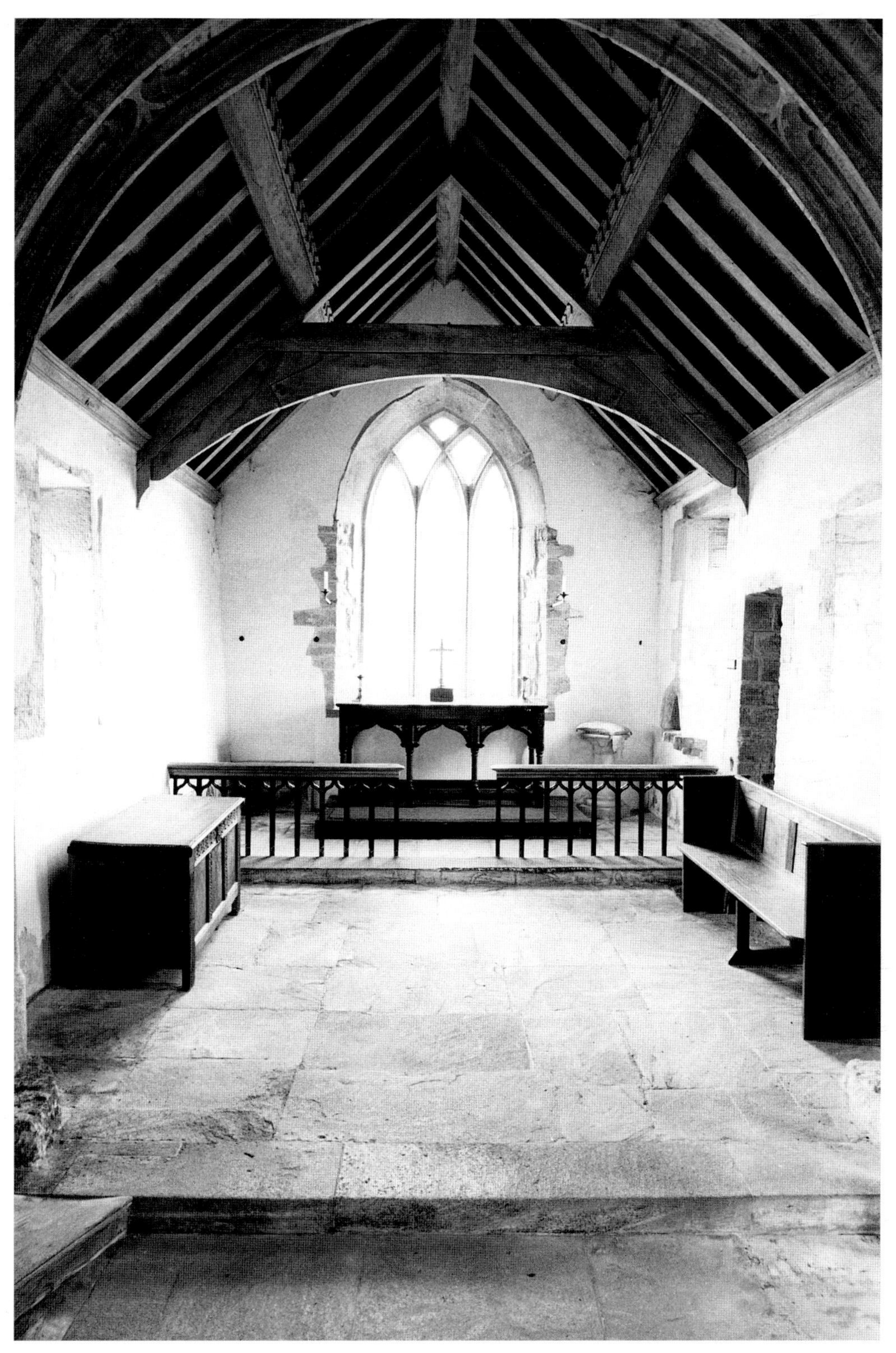

St. James, Interior, Chillington, Somerset by Denise Owen

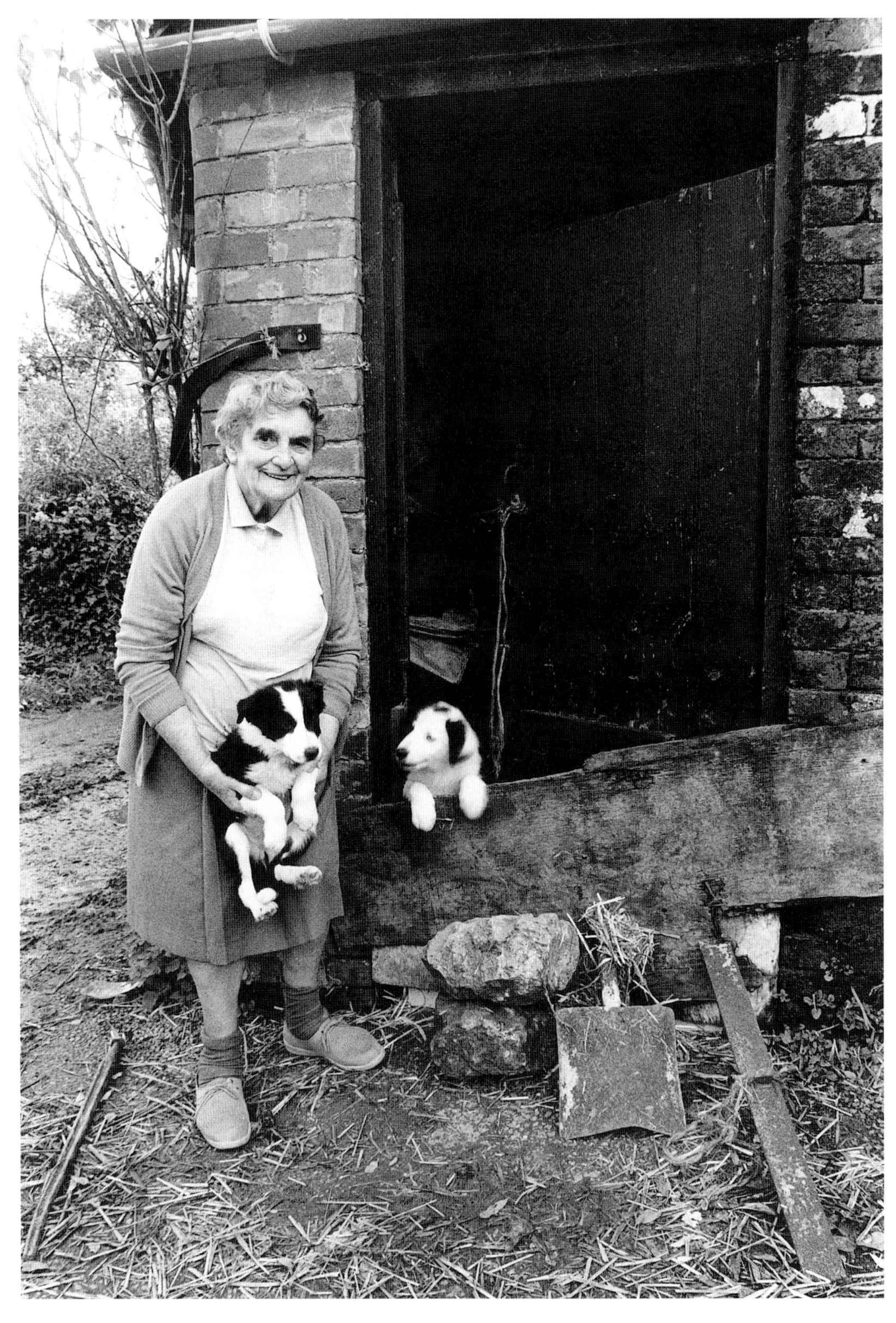

Mrs. Wyatt with collie pups, Cudworth, Somerset, by Nicky Saunter

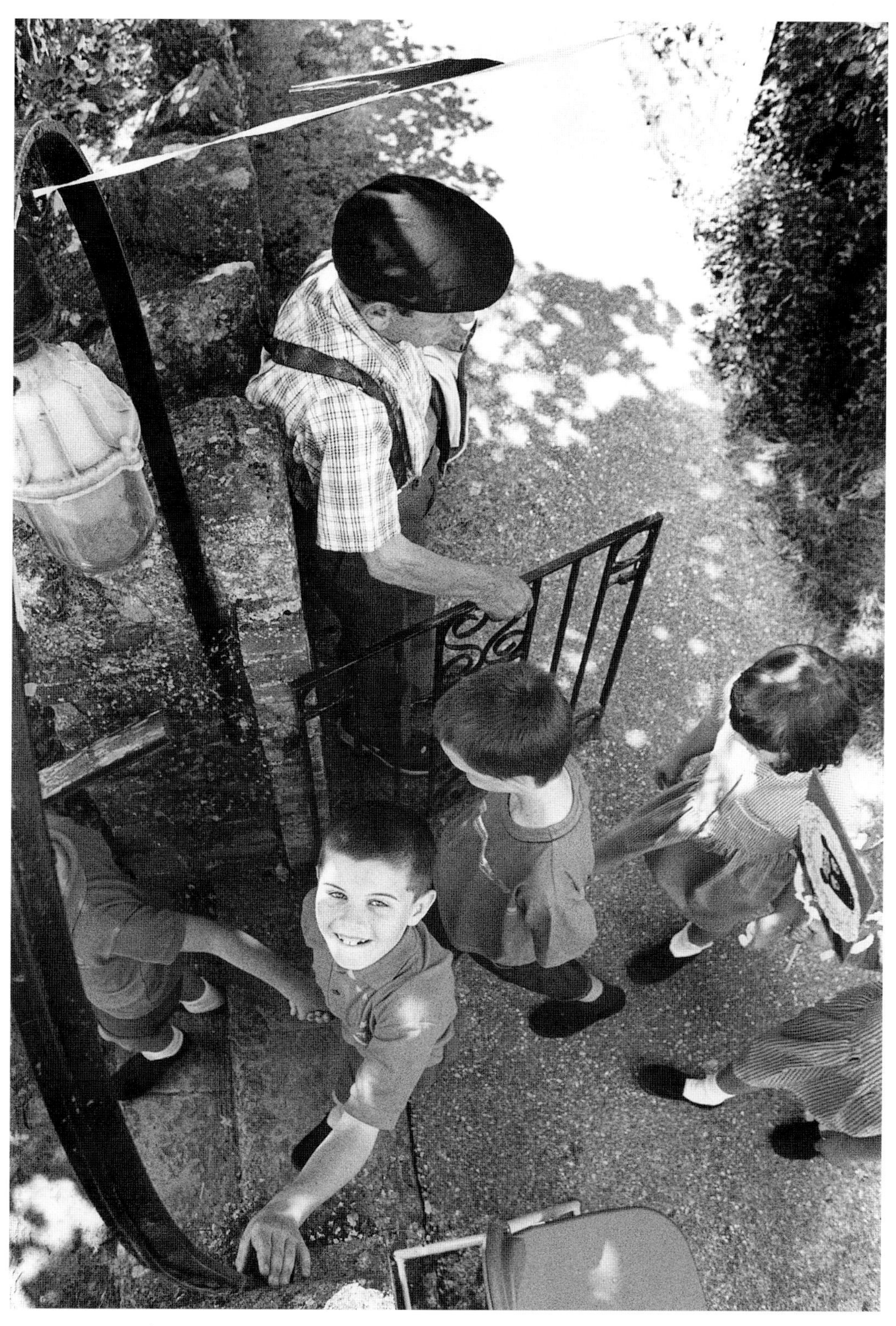

Children, Vicarage Garden, Shepton Beauchamp, Somerset by Nicky Saunter

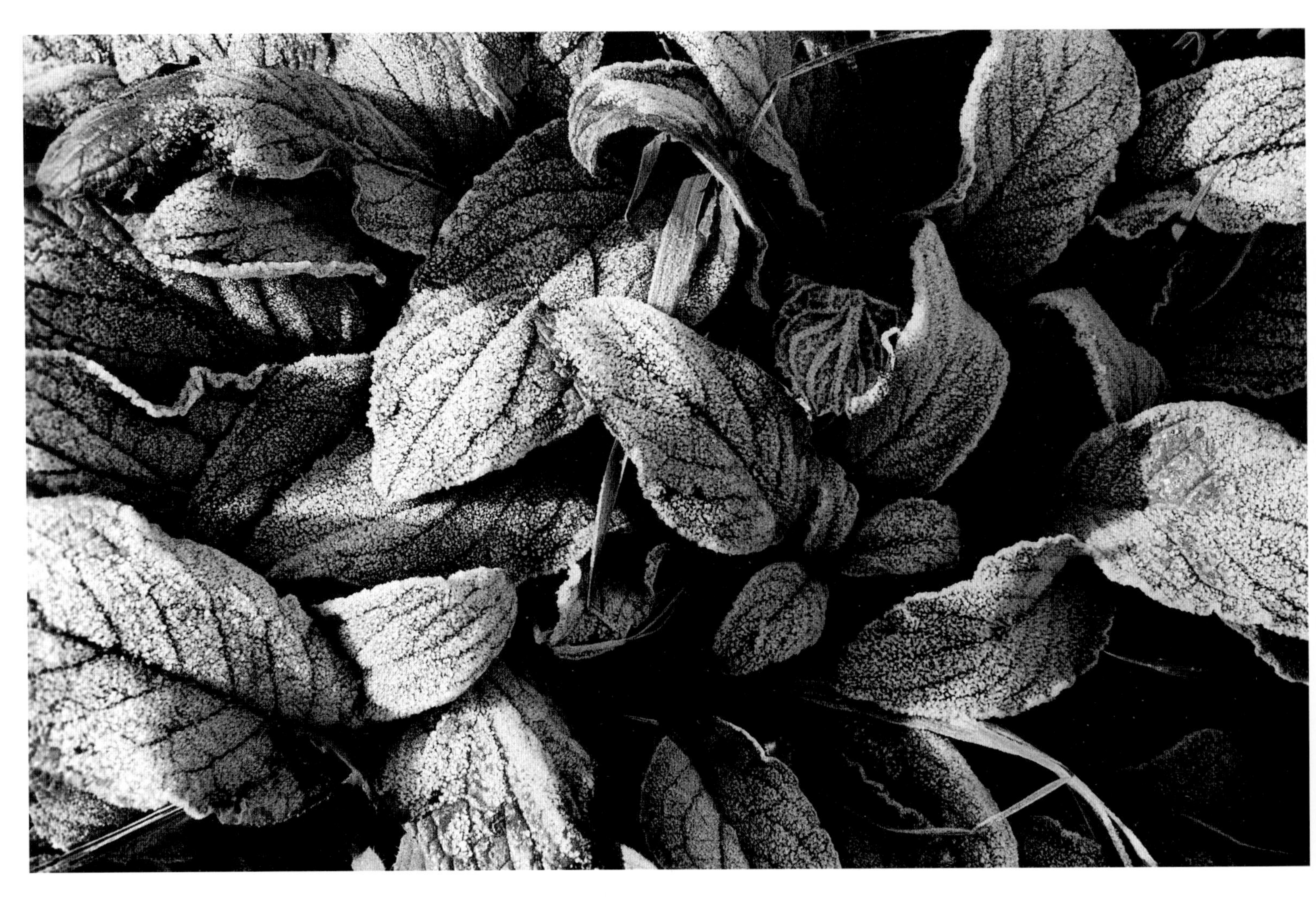

Frosted Leaves, Somerset by Sue Milverton

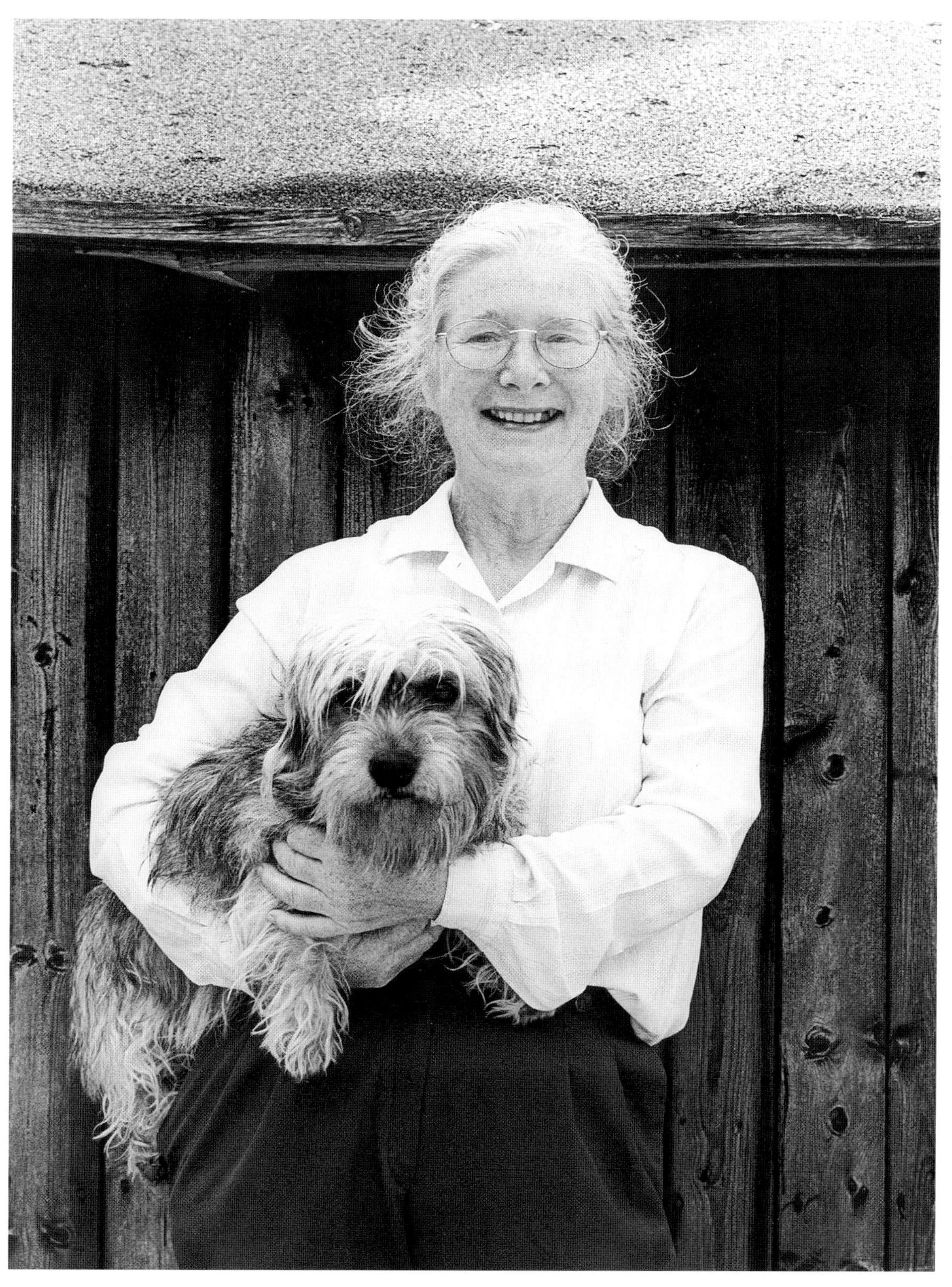

Rachel Webb and Happy, Dowlish Wake, Somerset by Sue Milverton

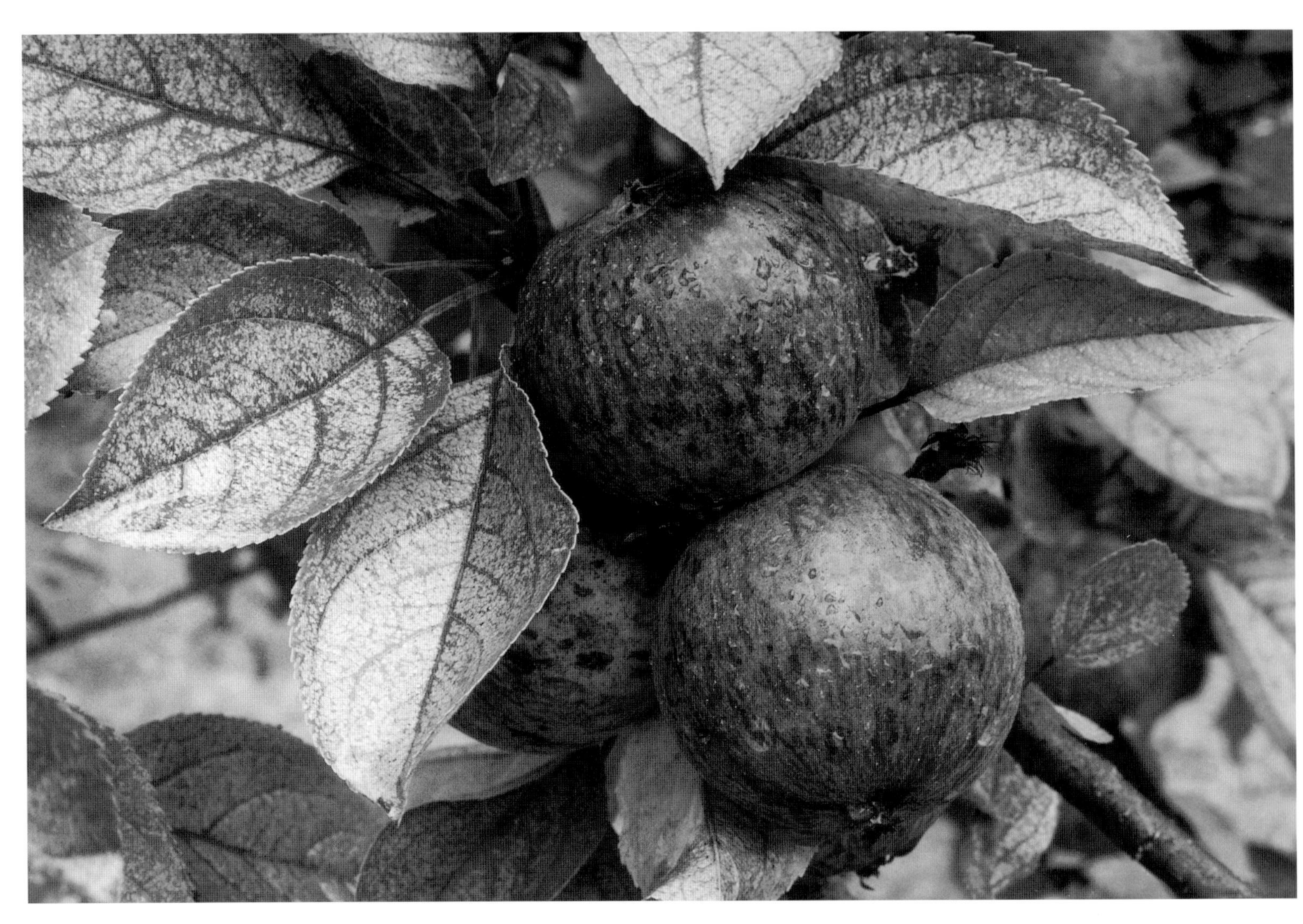

Dabinett Cider Apples, Knowle St. Giles, Somerset by Liz Perry

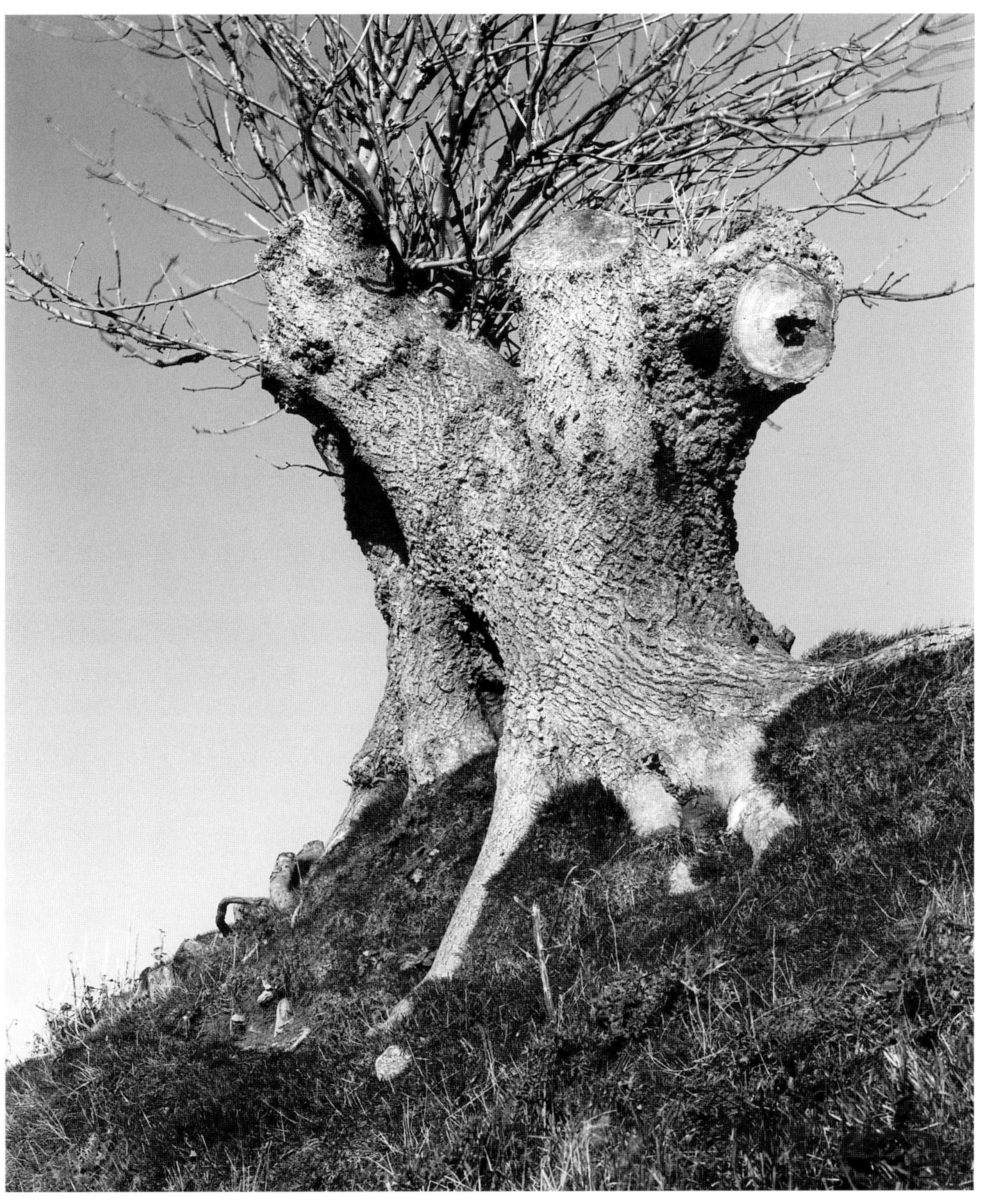

Ash Tree, Ham Hill, Somerset, by Jerry Mitchell

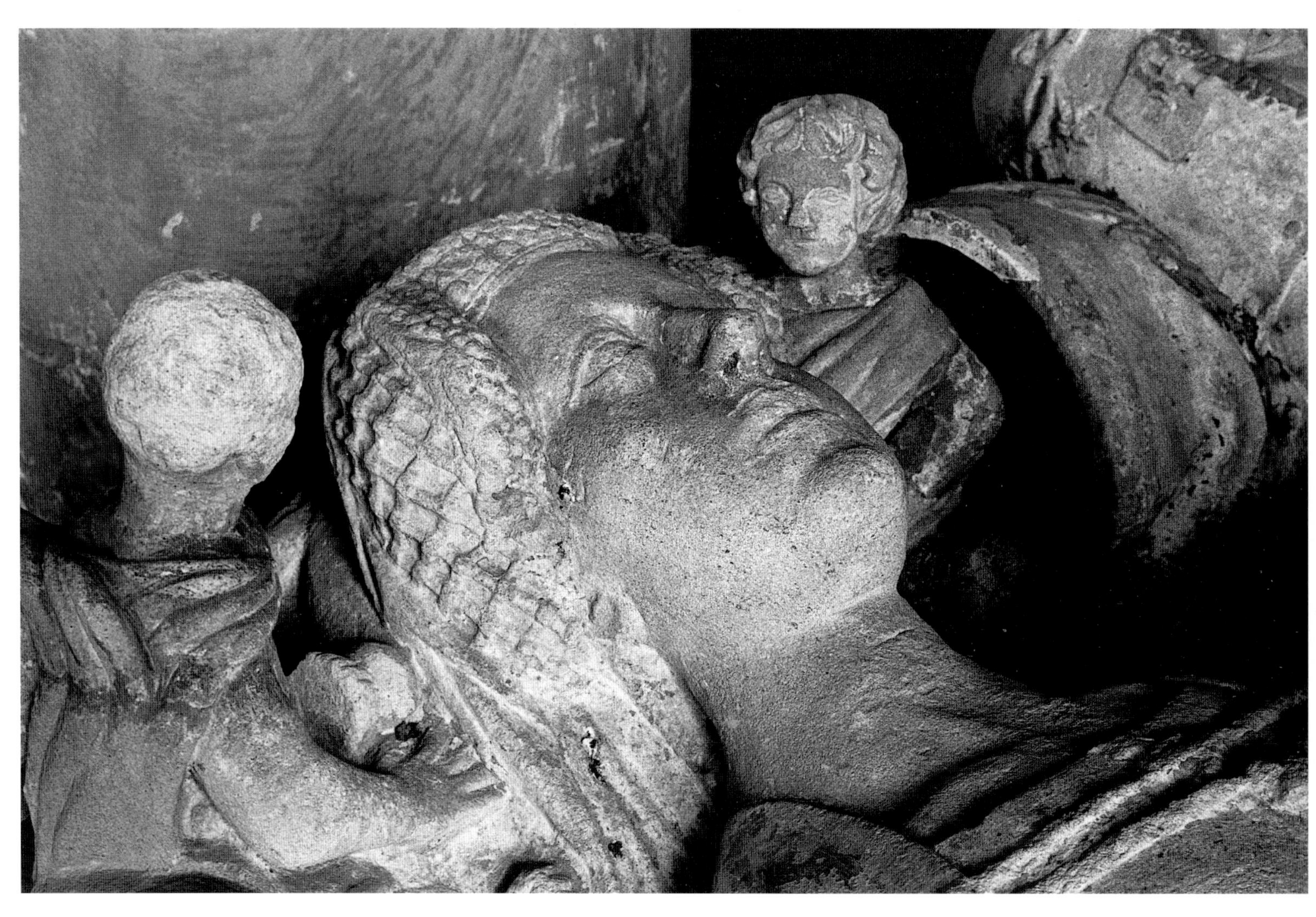

Effigy, St. Thomas of Canterbury Church, Cothelstone, Somerset by Christopher Rimmer

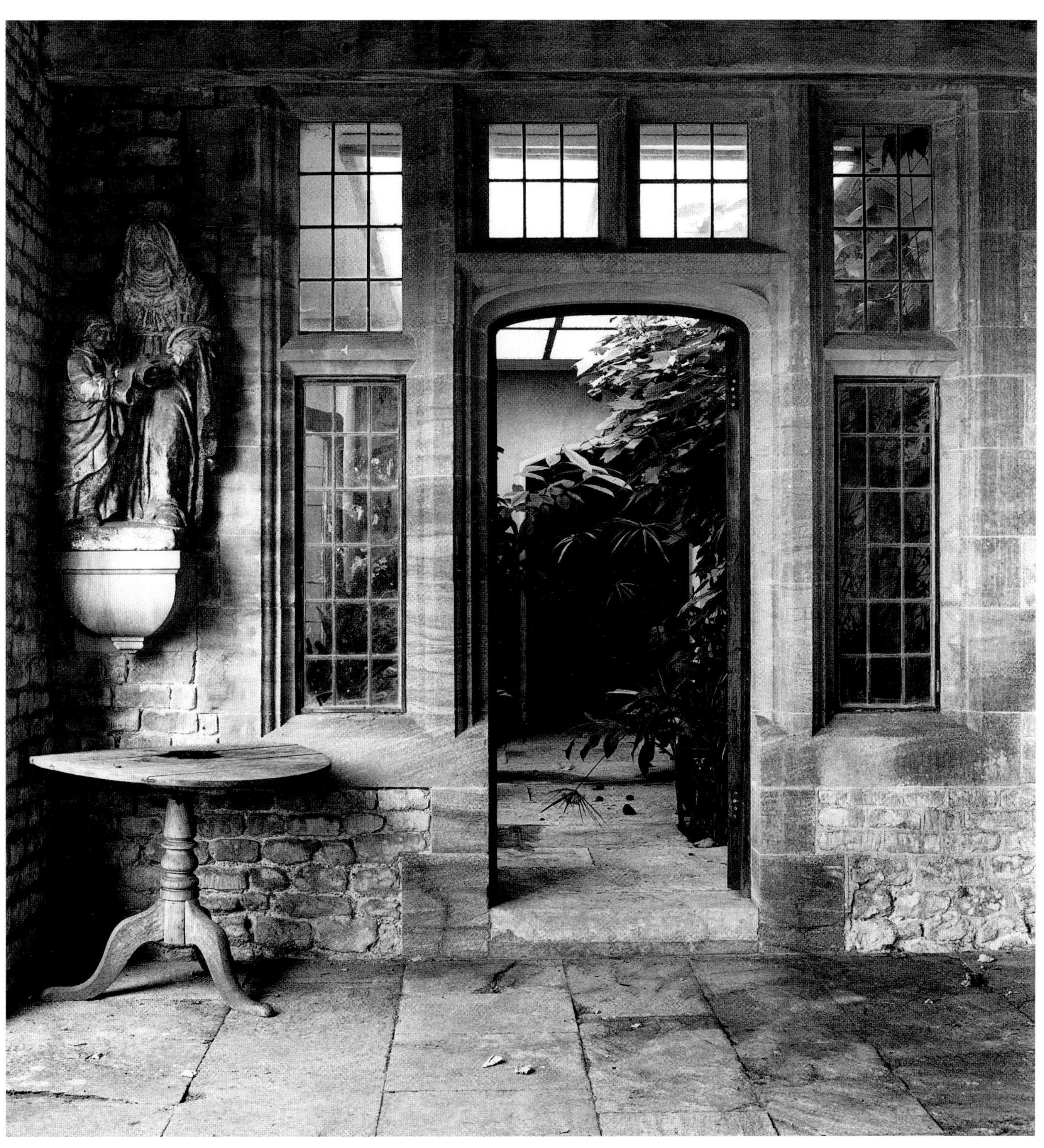

The Conservatory, Wayford Manor, Somerset by Christopher Rimmer

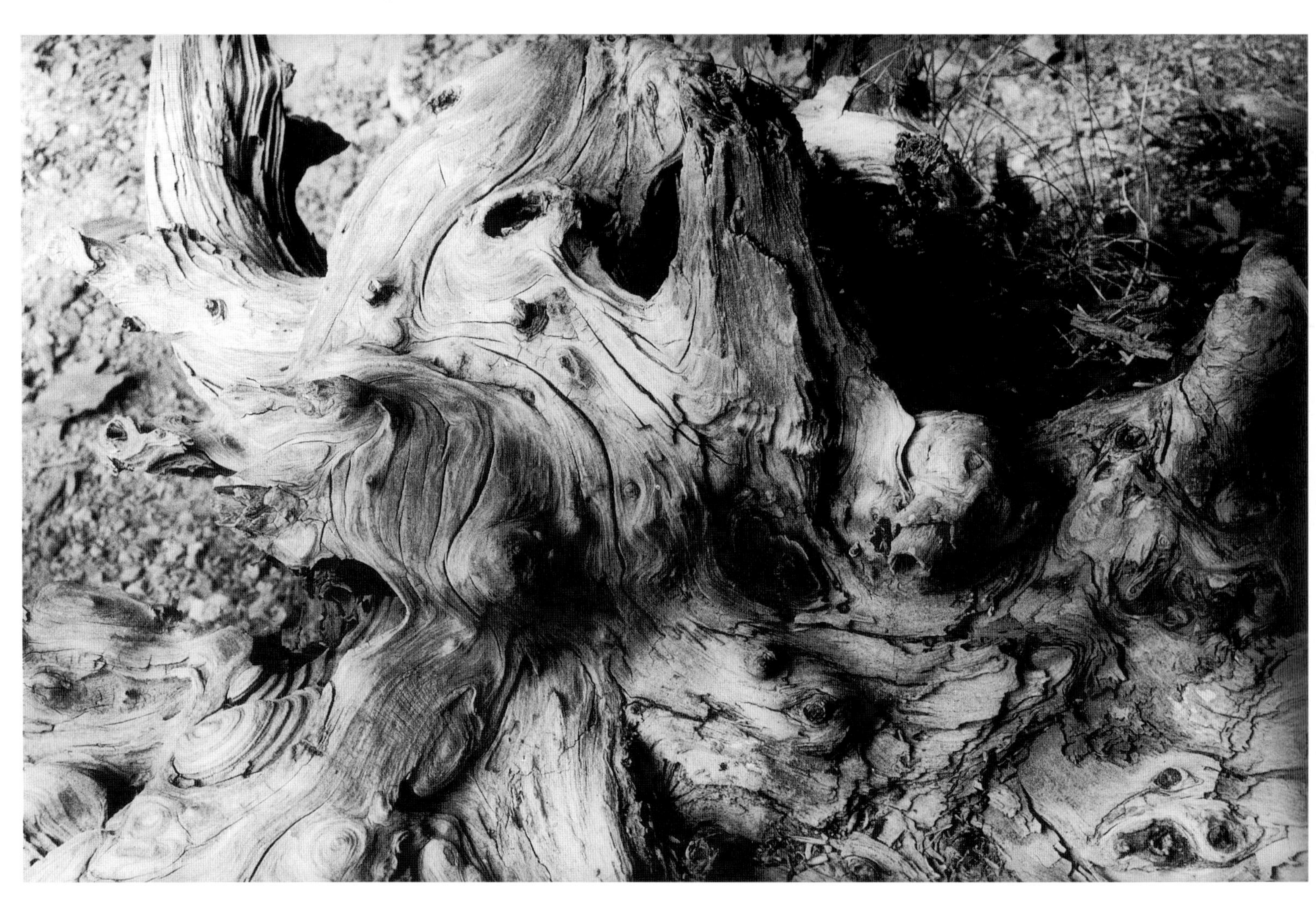

Gnarled Wood, Somerset by Natasha Greig

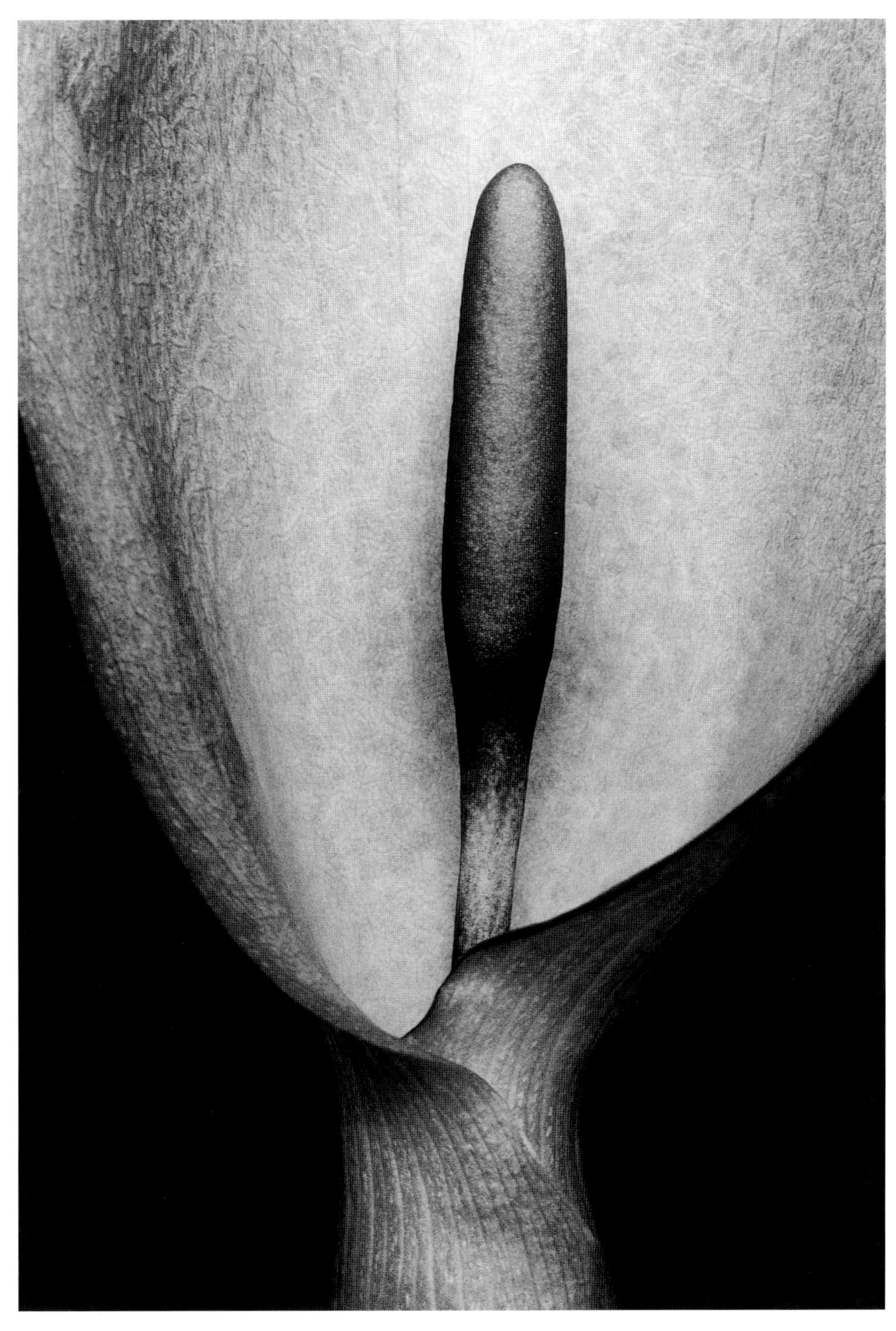

Lords and Ladies, Devon by Carol Green

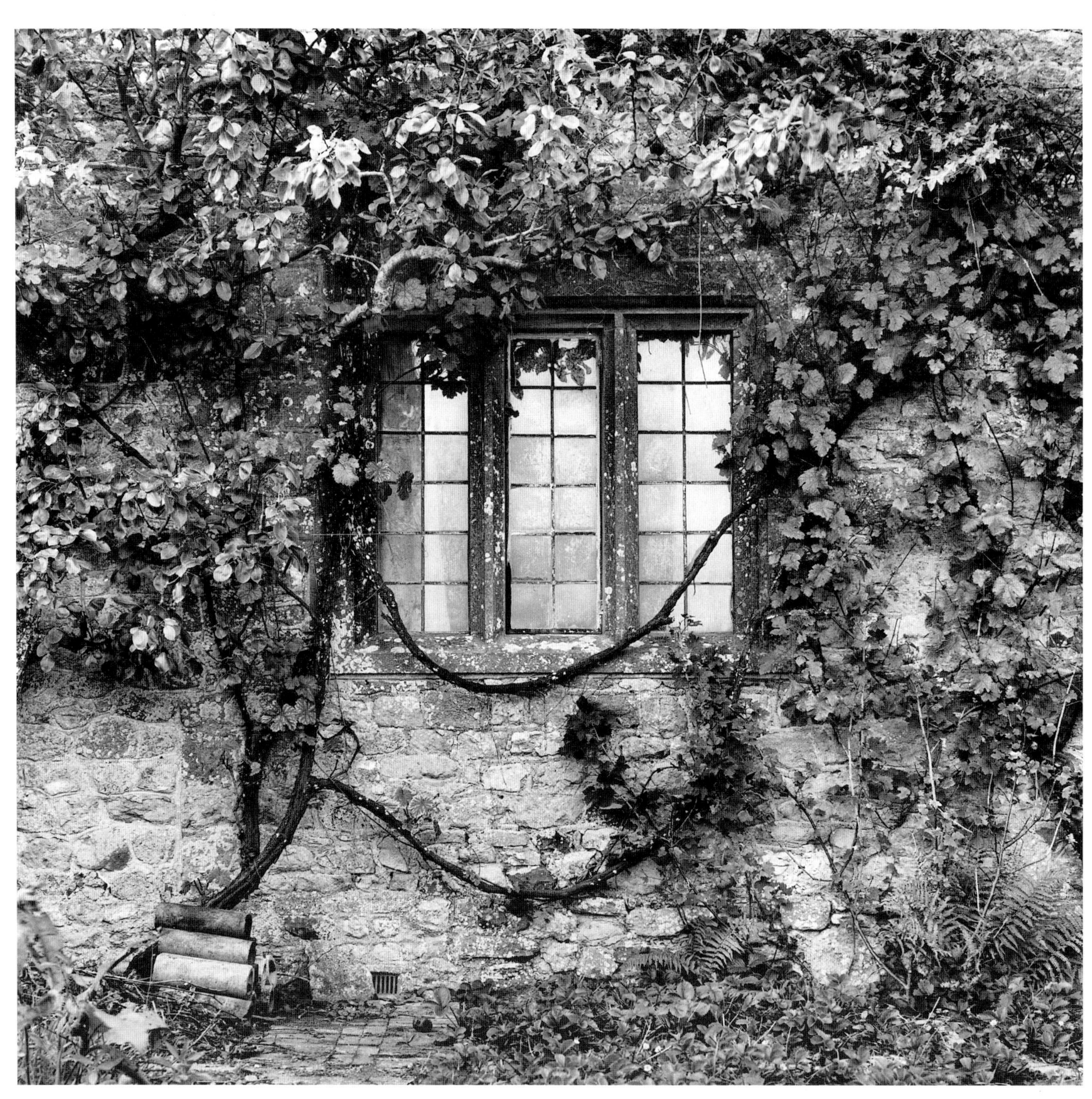

Window, Wayford Manor, Somerset by Christopher Rimmer

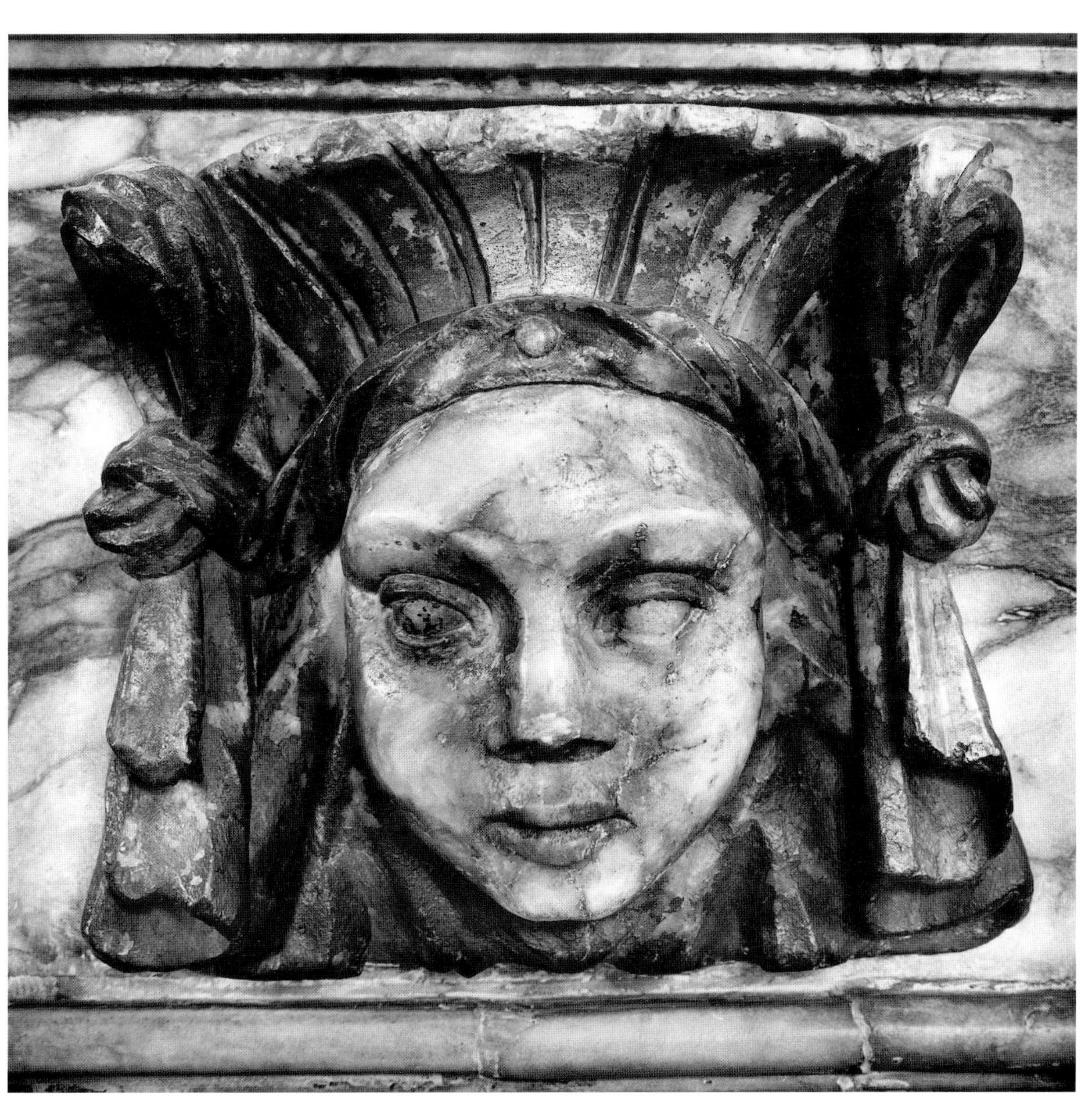

Pillar Decoration, St. Peter and St. Paul's, Bishops Hull, Somerset by Stan Ashcroft

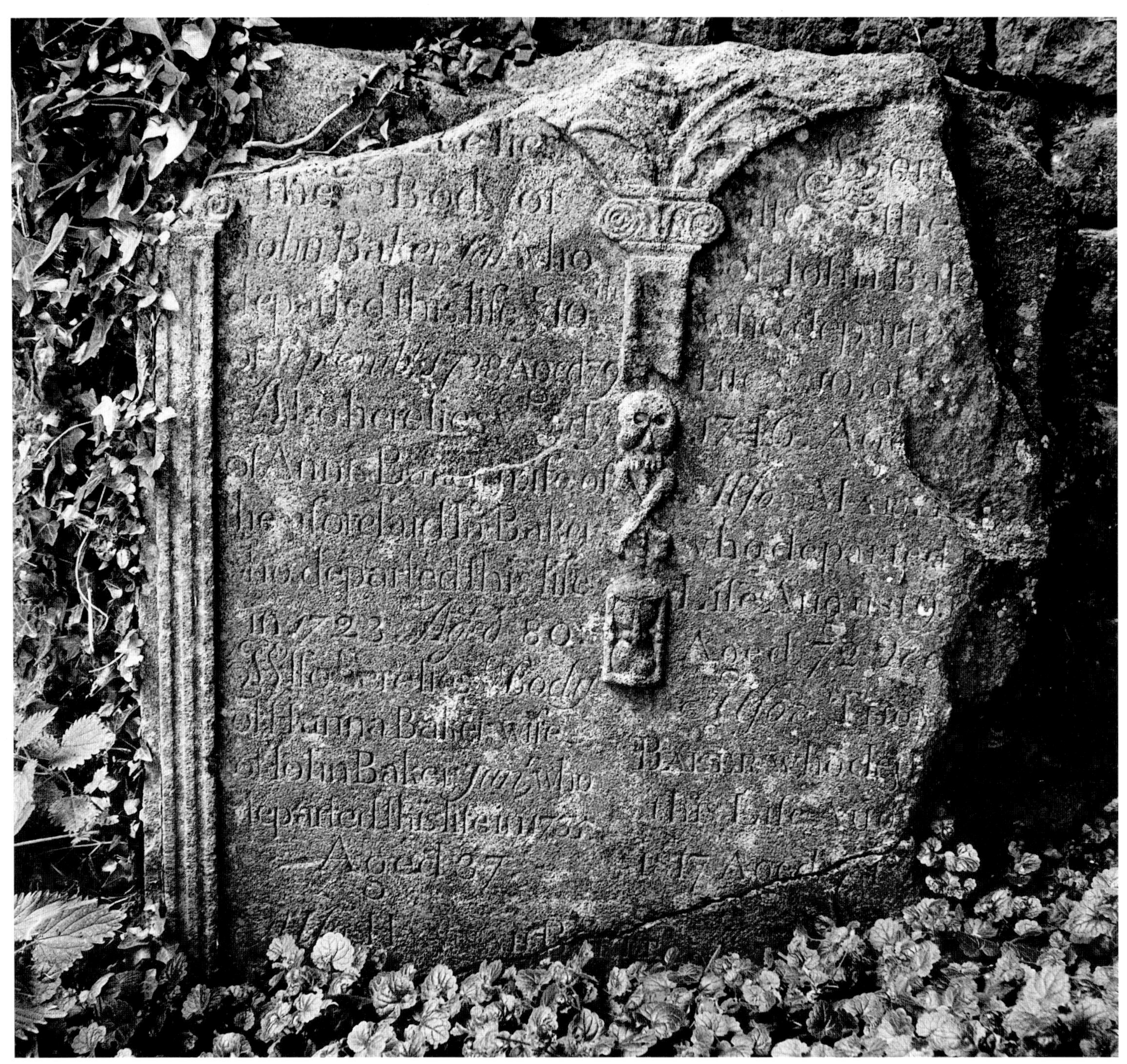

Gravestone and Ivy, St. Andrew, Puckington, Somerset by Sue Milverton

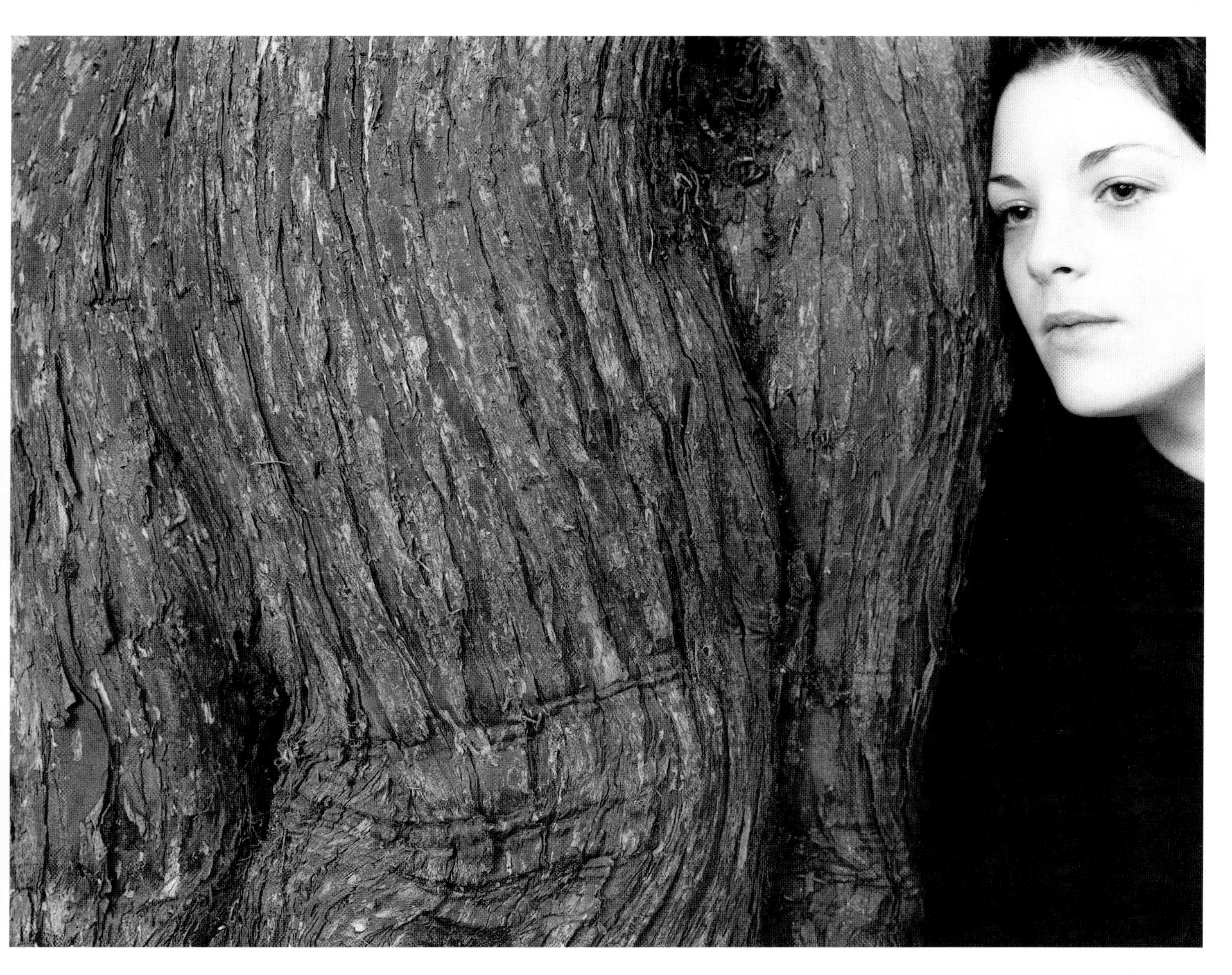

Louise in the Wilderness, Dillington House, Somerset, by Paul Harvey

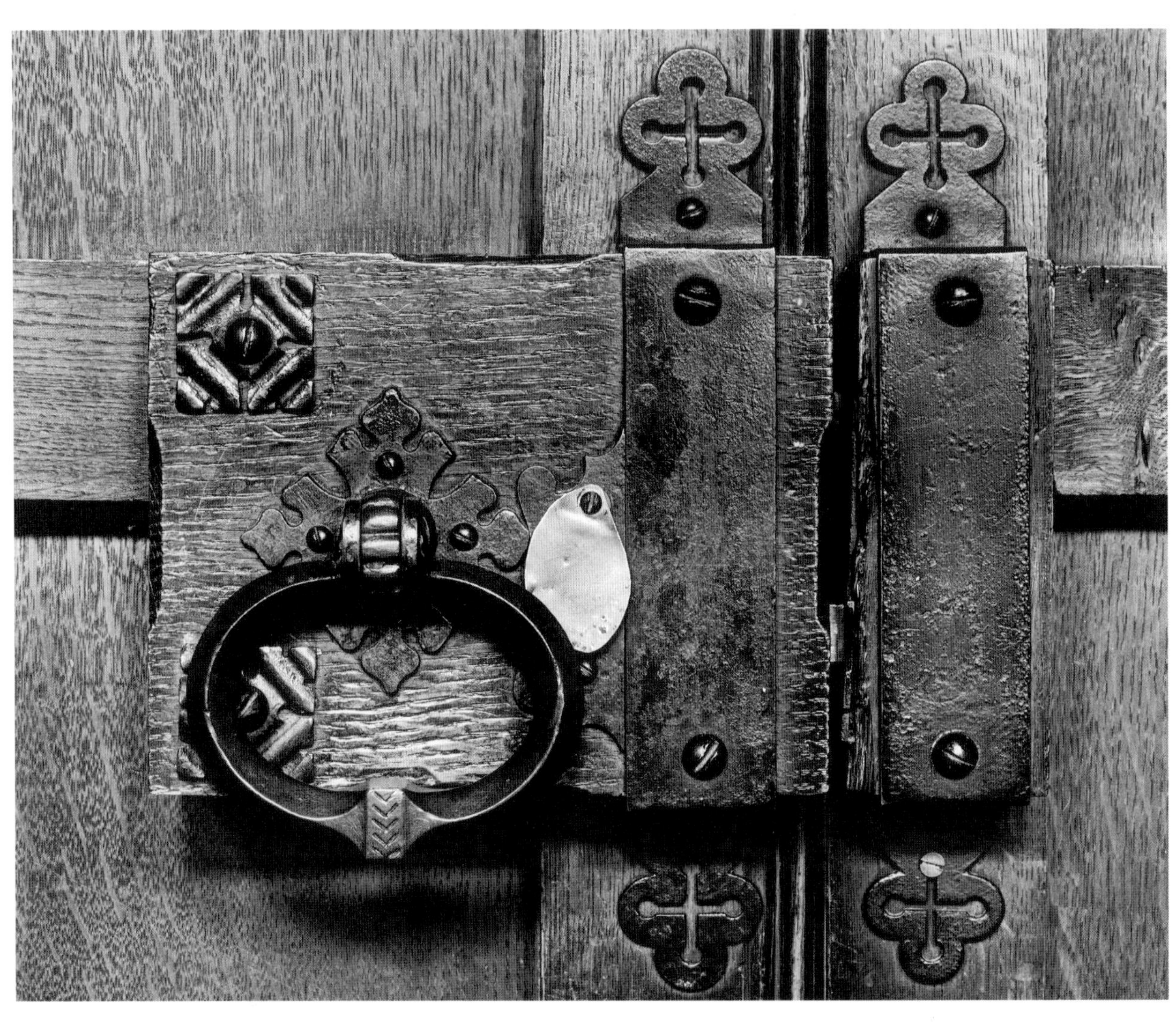

Lock, North Door, St. Michael and All Angels, Somerton, Somerset by Stan Ashcroft

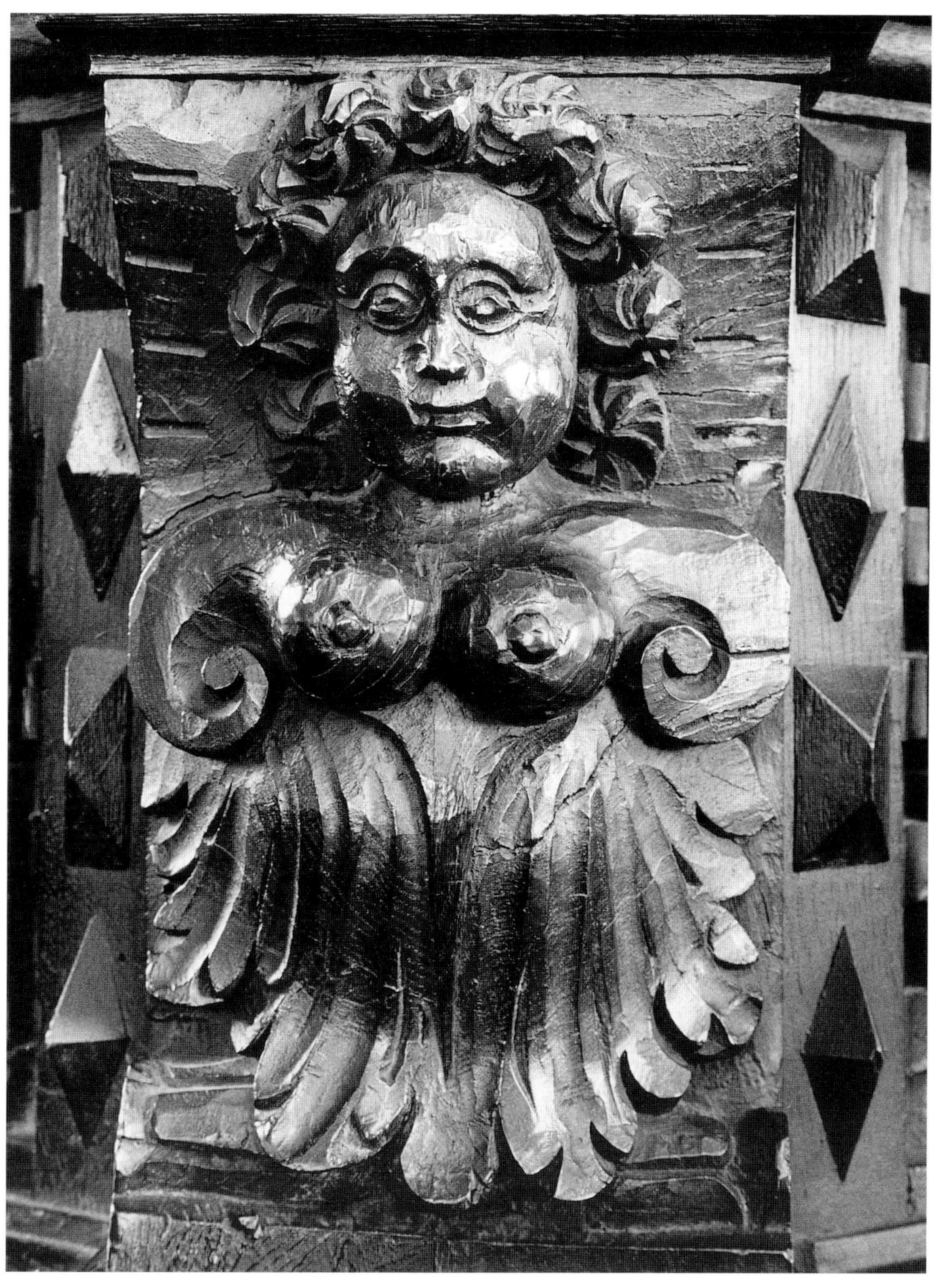

Carving of a Woman, Pulpit, St. Cuthbert's, Wells, Somerset by Janet Carmichael

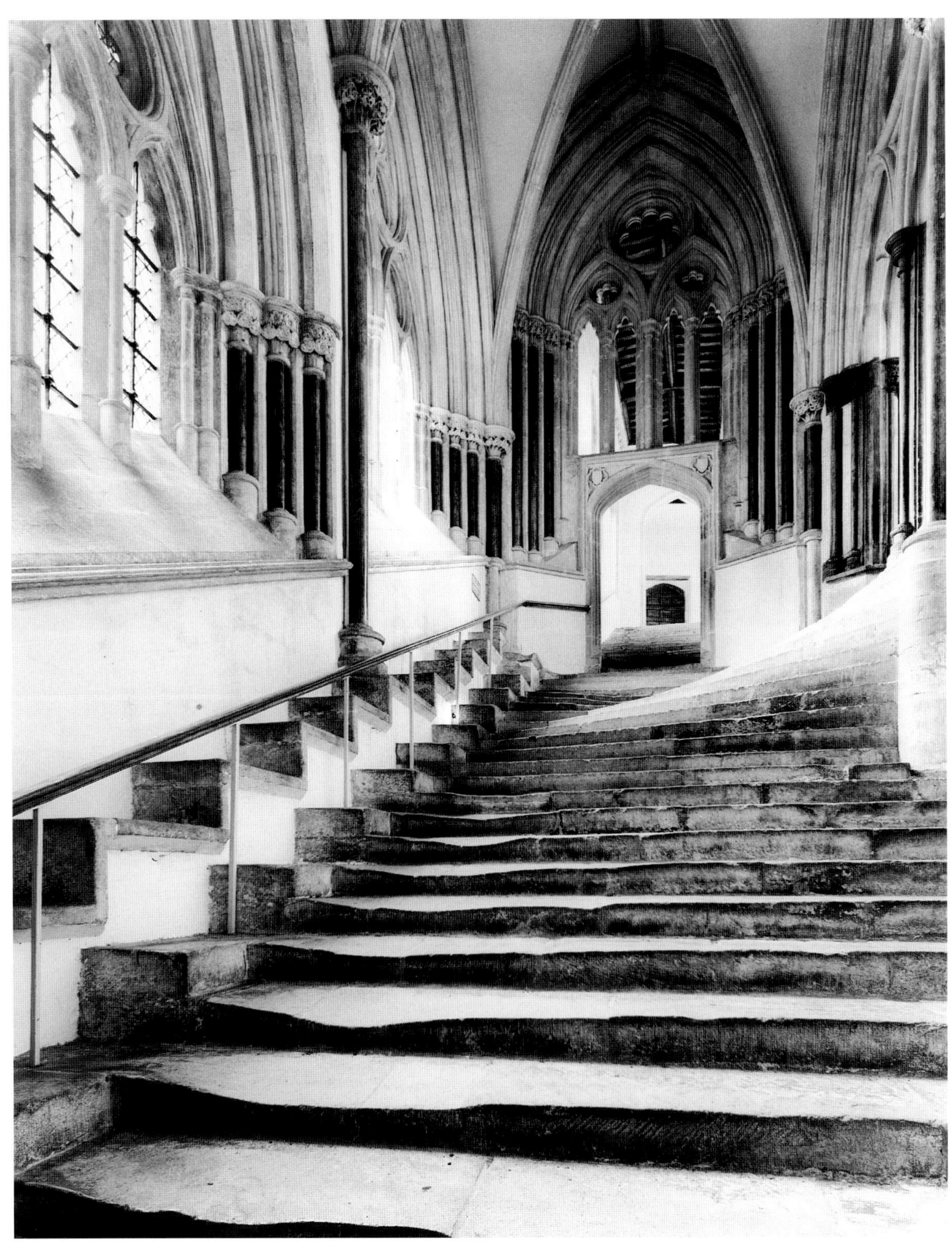

Chapter House Steps, Wells Cathedral, Somerset by Ulick Palmer

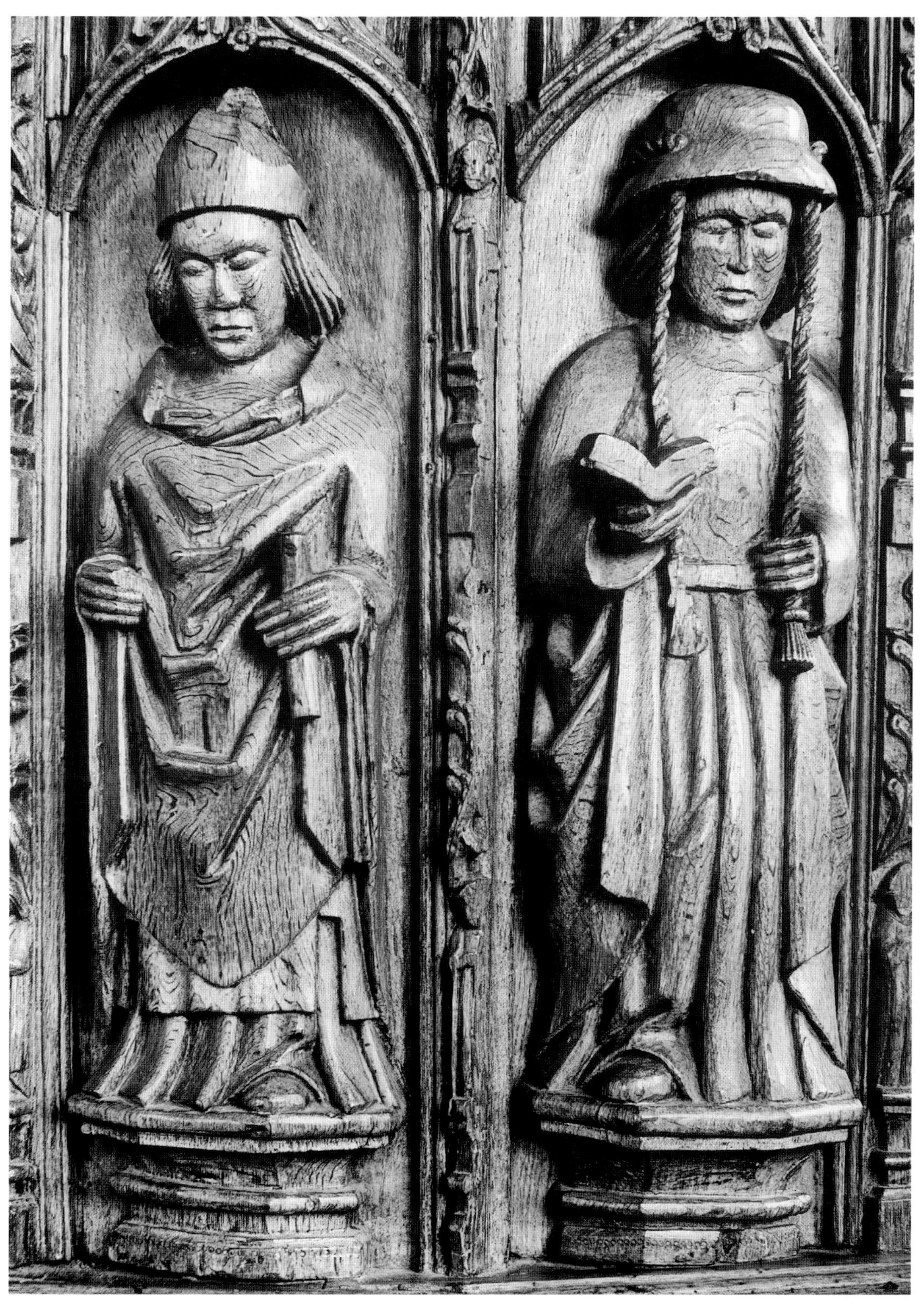

Pulpit Detail, All Saints', Trull, Somerset by Stan Ashcroft

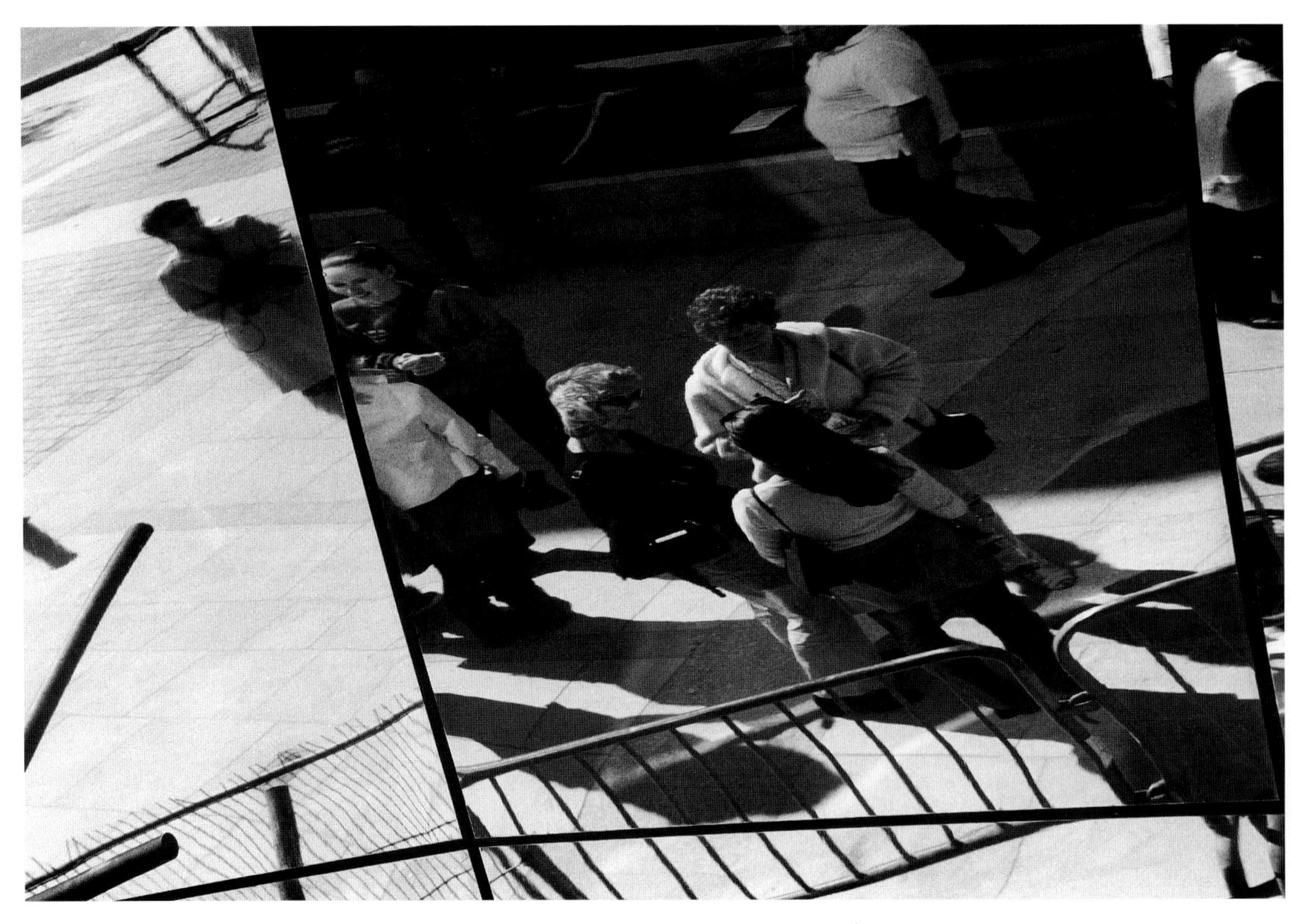

Urban Reflections, Somerset by Peter Hill

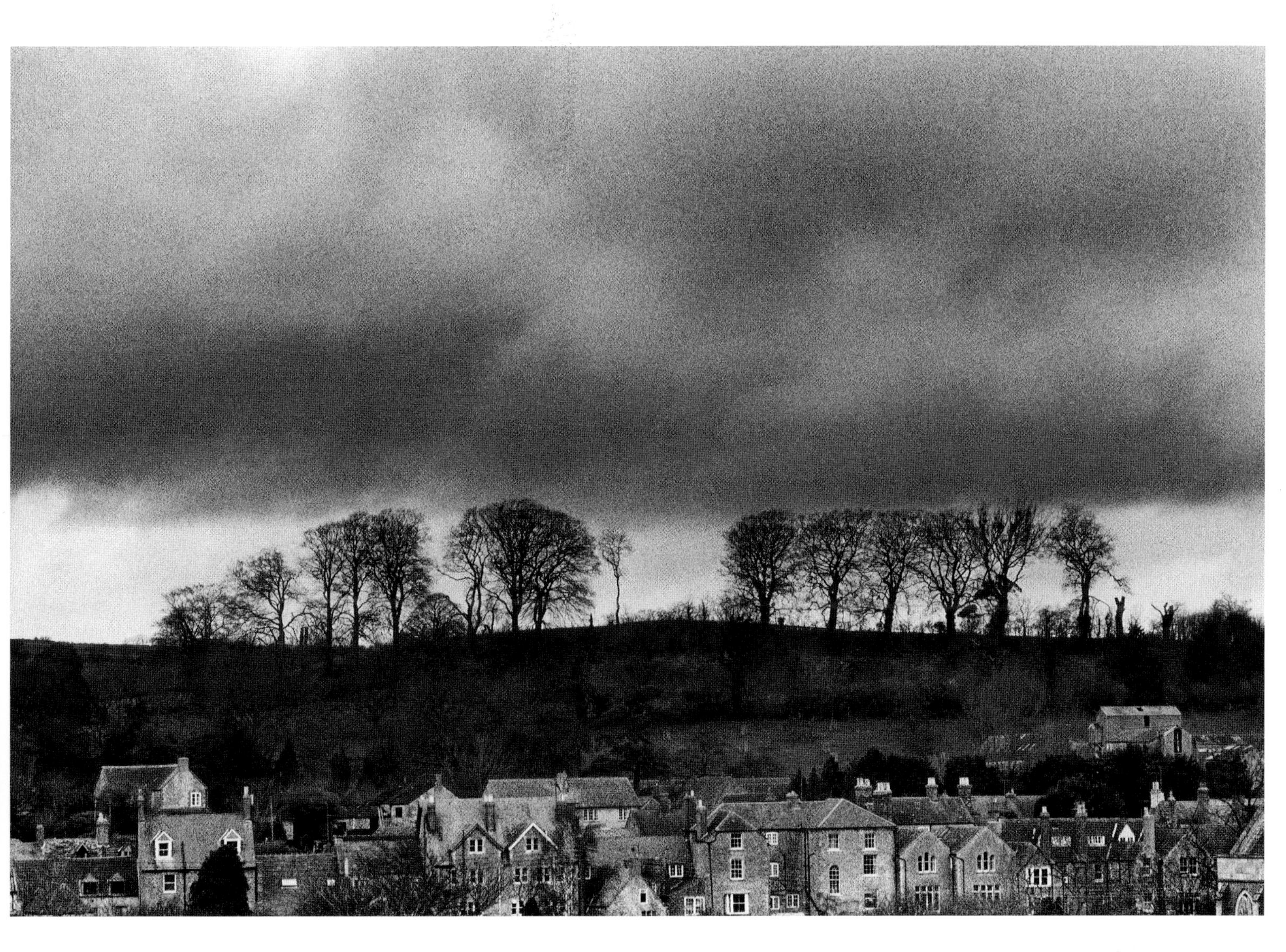

Bruton, Somerset by Vicky Taylor

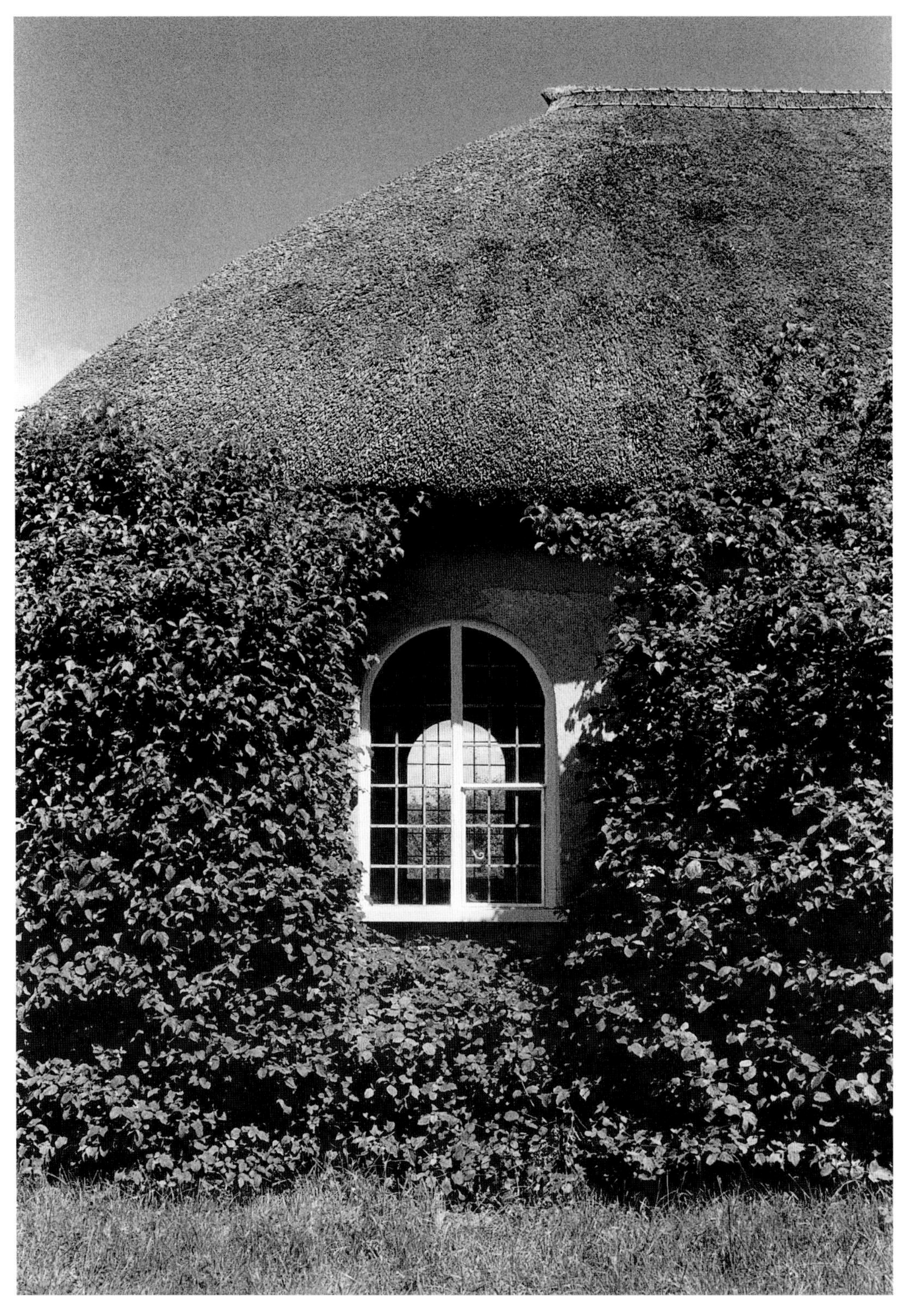

Loughwood Meeting House, Exterior, Kilmington, Devon by Denise Owen

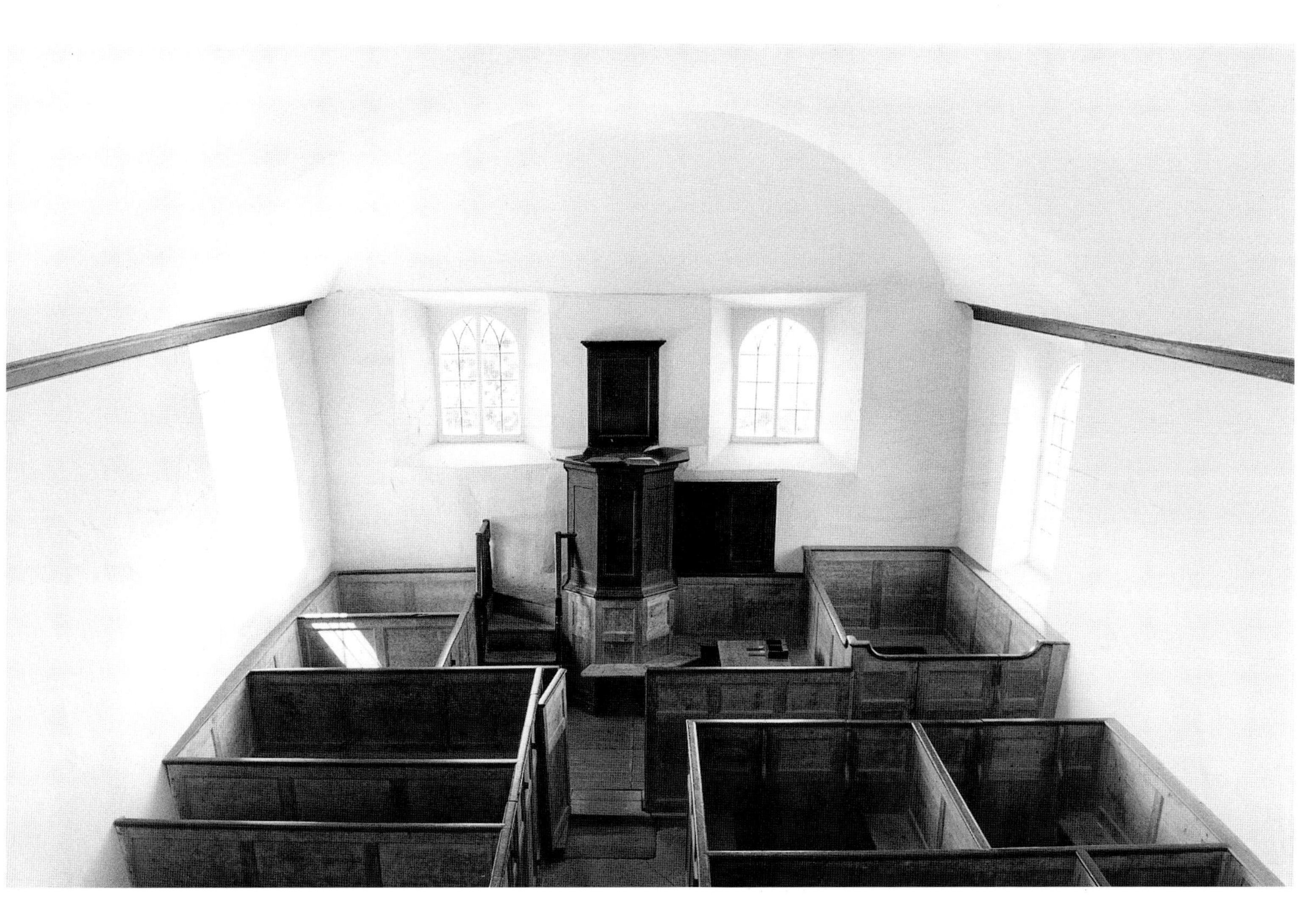

Loughwood Meeting House, Interior, Kilmington, Devon by Denise Owen

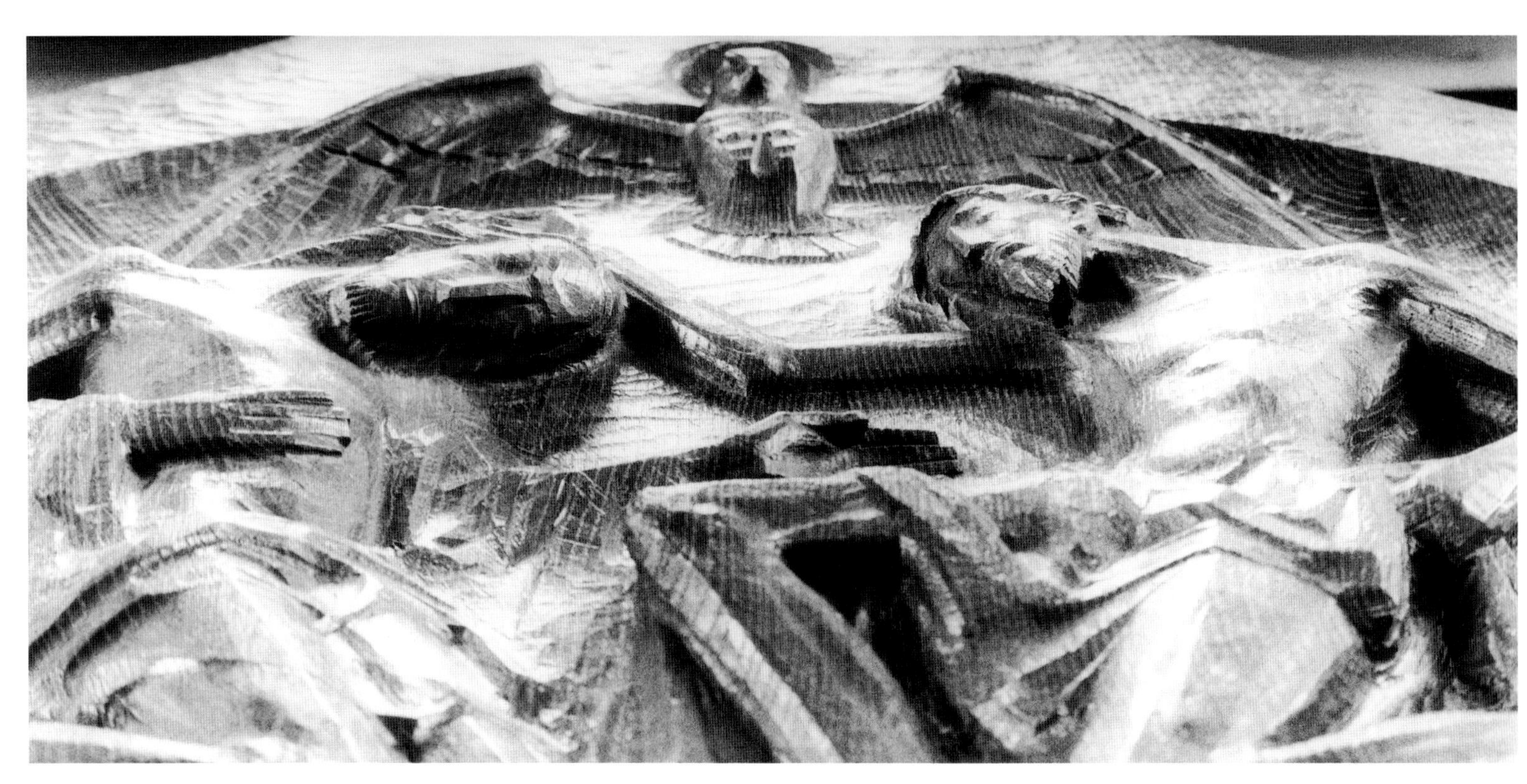

Font Cover, The Minster Church of St. Mary the Virgin, Axminster, Devon by Nathan Glover

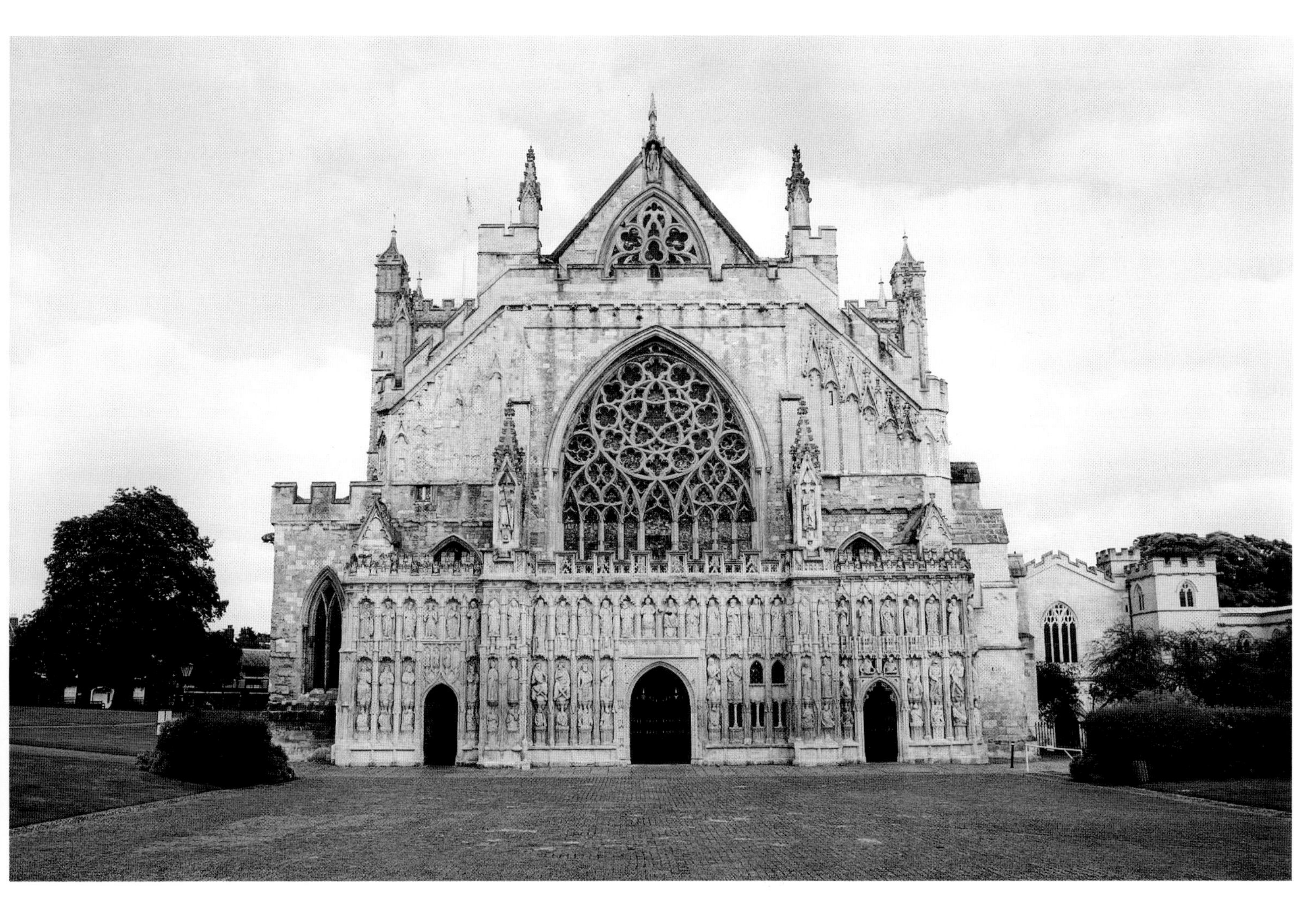

Exeter Cathedral, Exeter, Devon by Vicky West

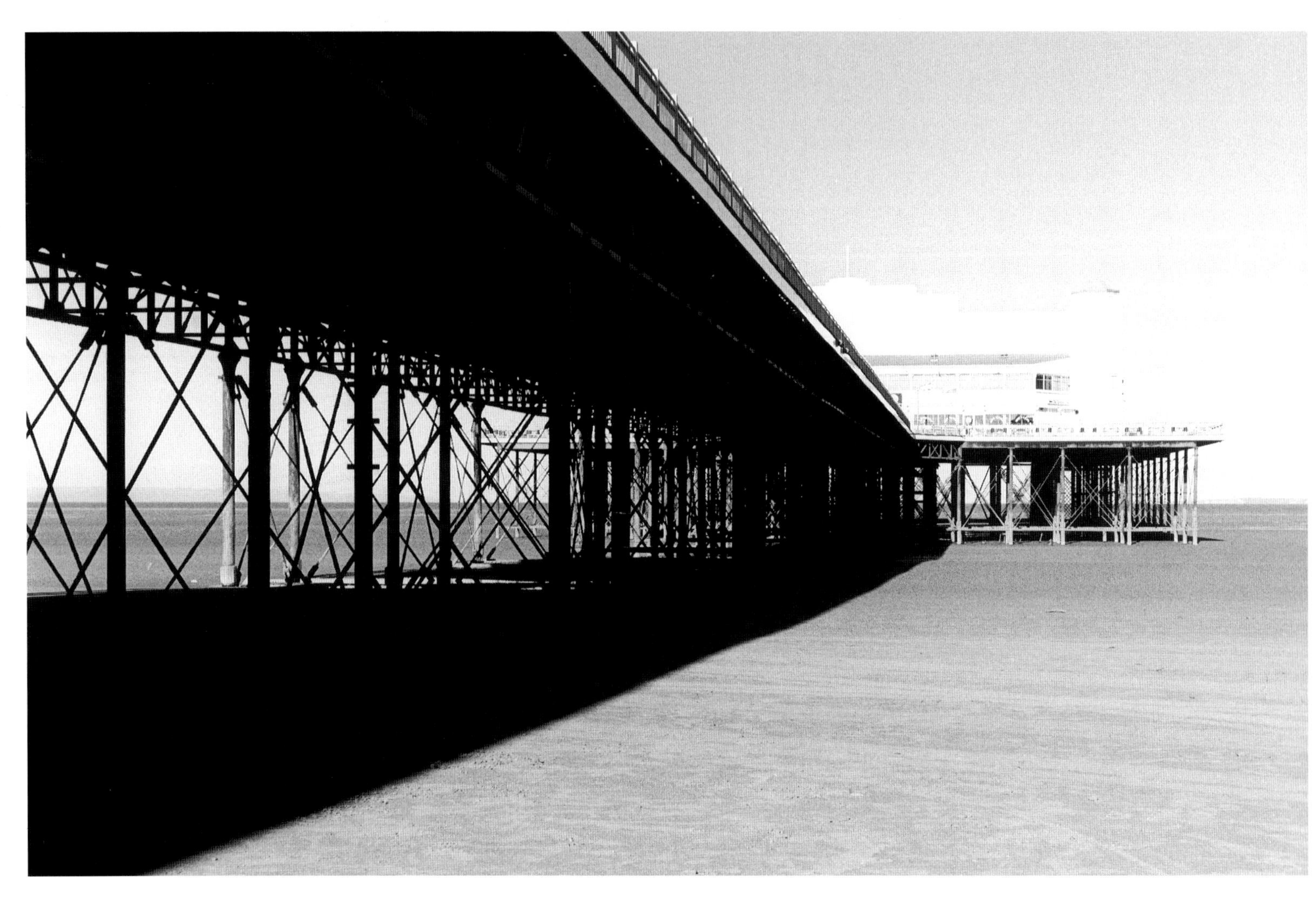

The Grand Pier, Weston-super-Mare, Somerset by Adrian Turton

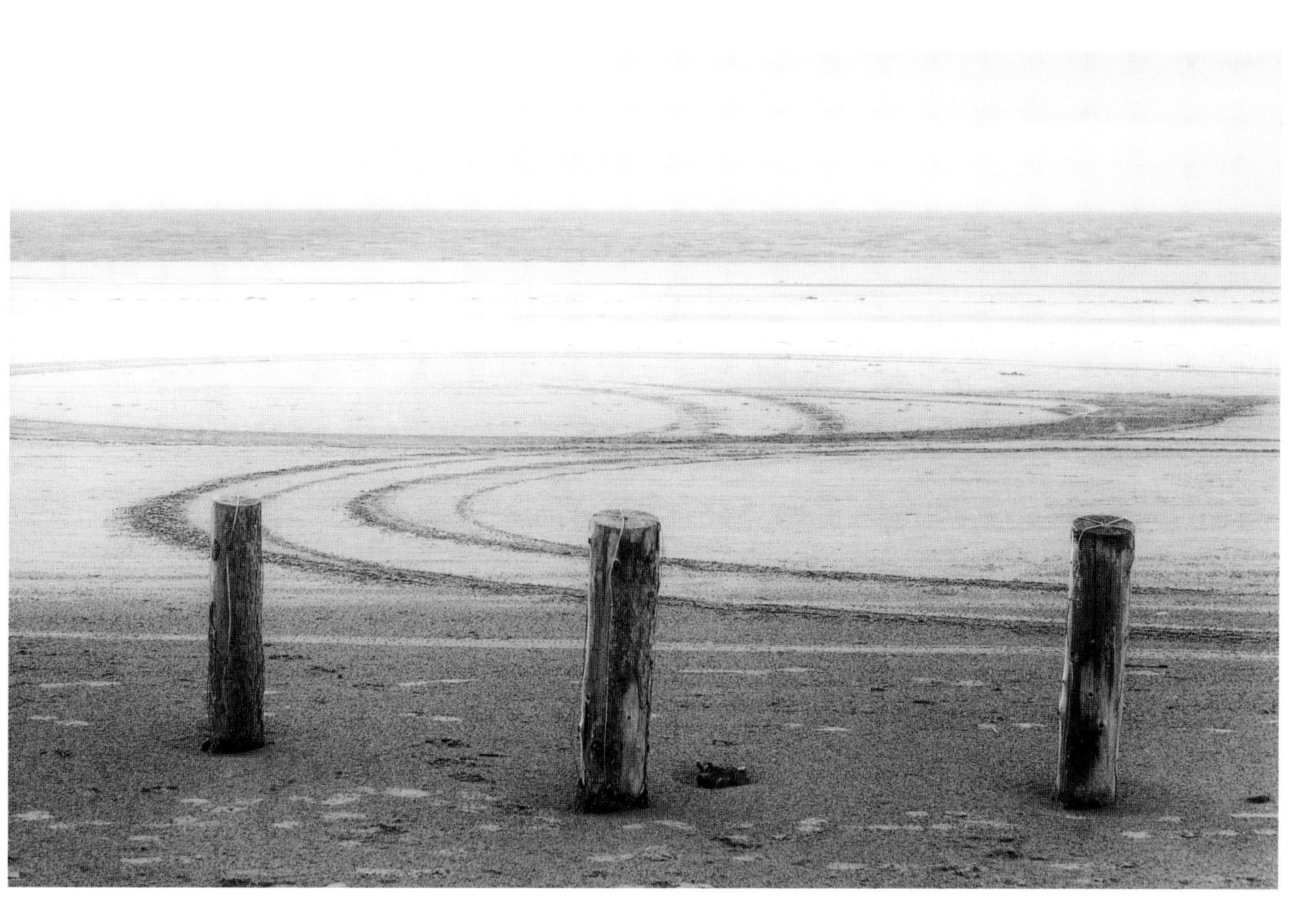

Posts, Berrow Beach, Somerset by Natasha Greig

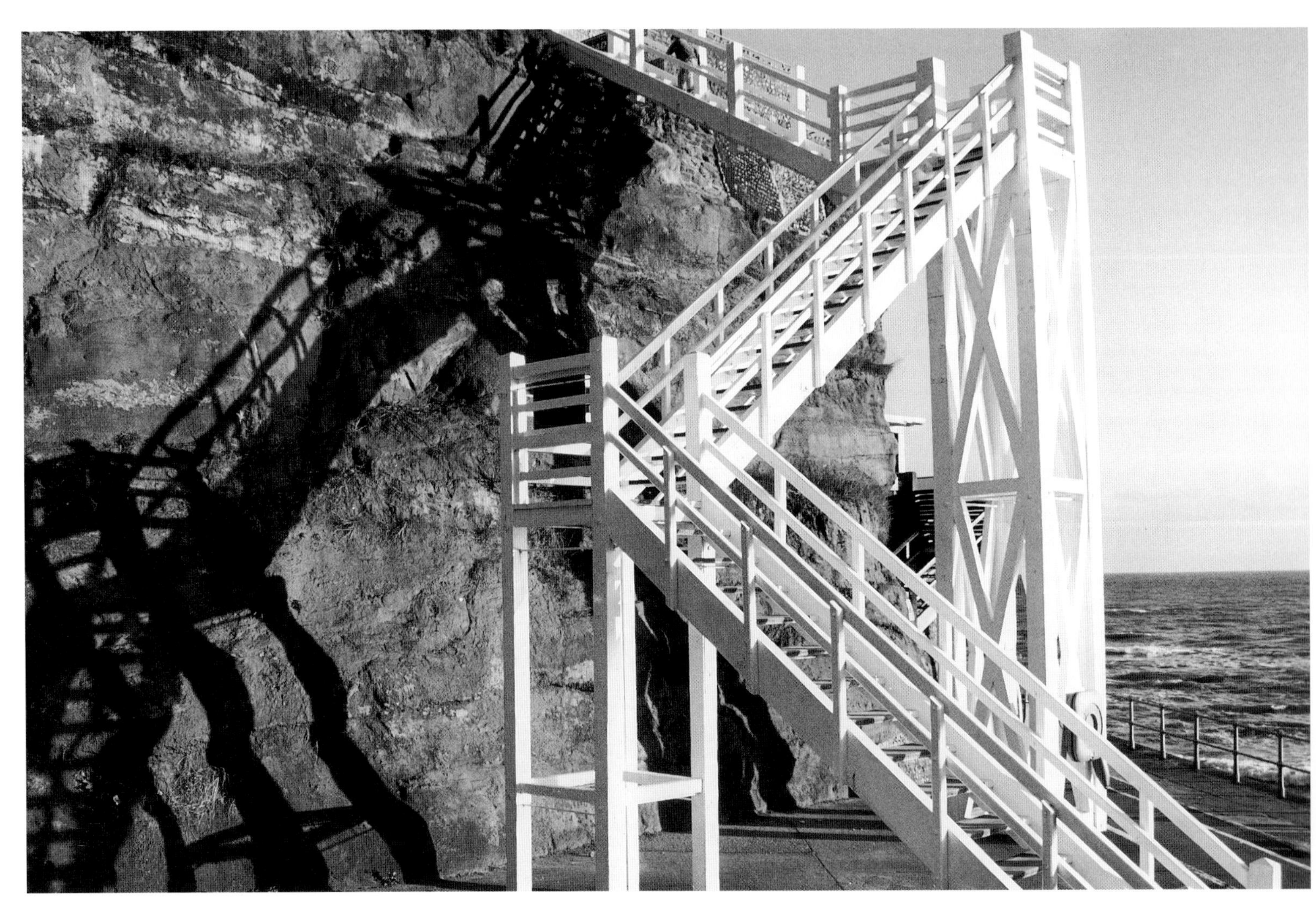

Jacob's Ladder, Sidmouth, Devon by Peter Livingstone

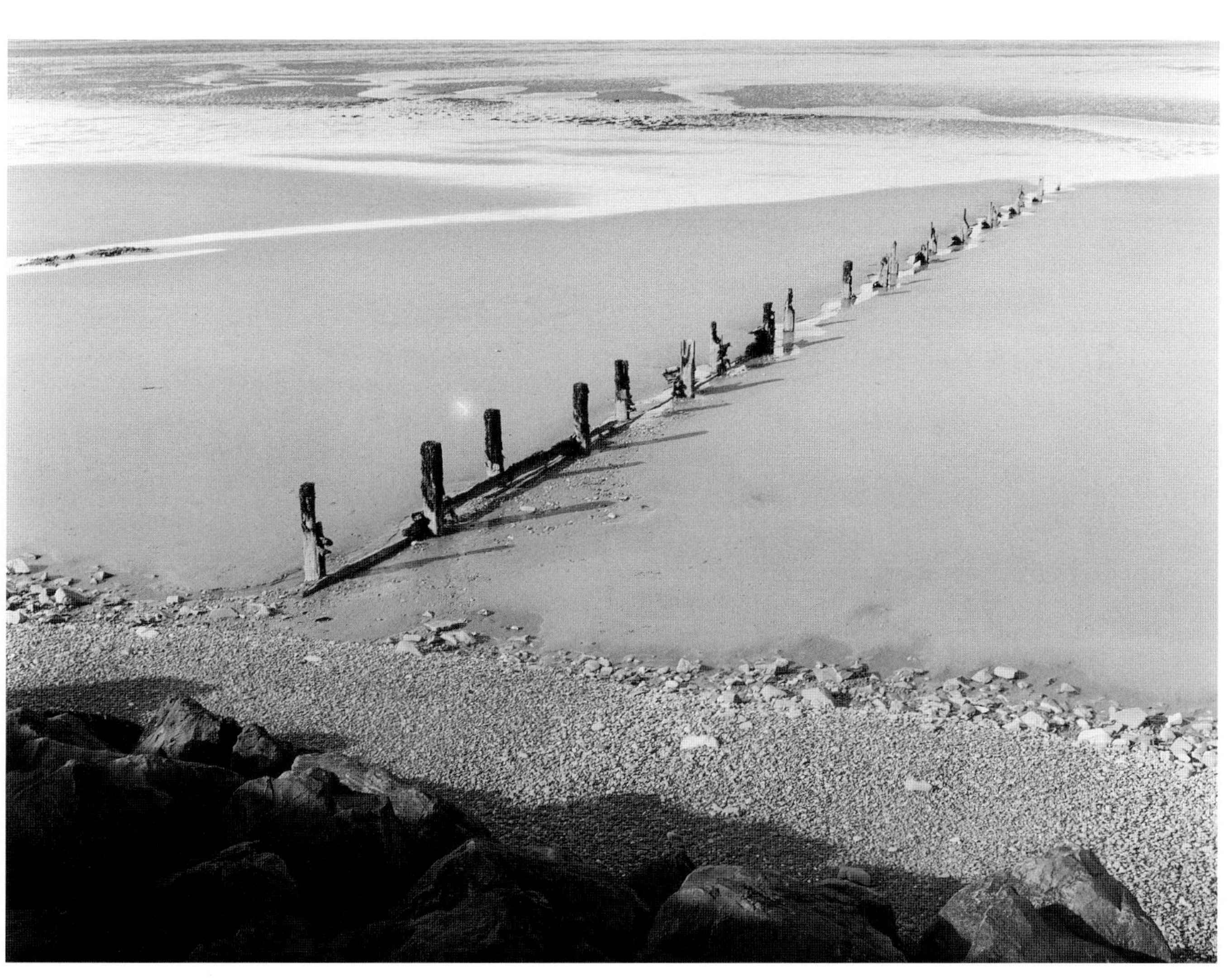

Seascape, North Somerset by Gordon Hall

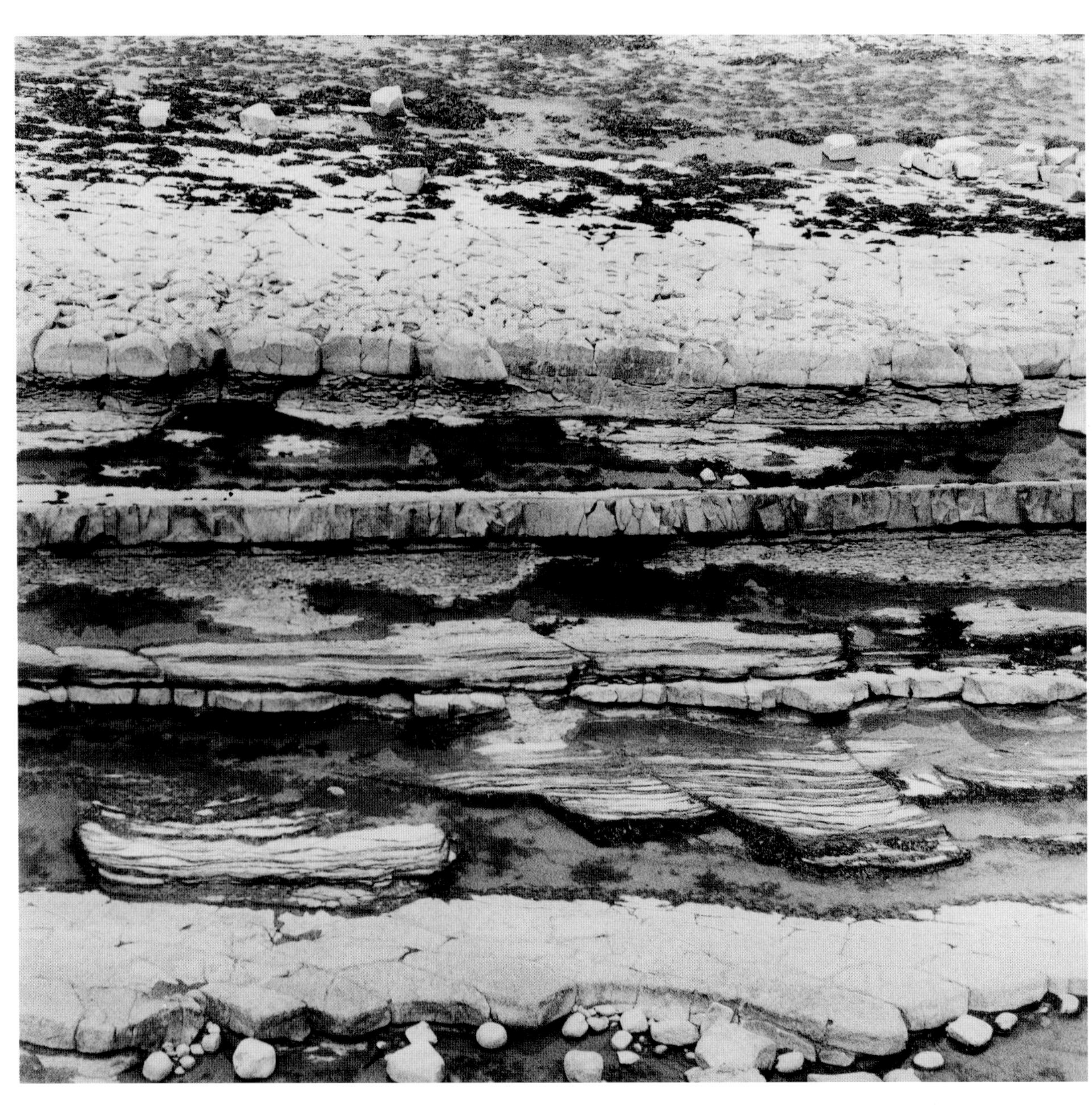

Rock Strata, Kilve, Somerset by Natasha Greig

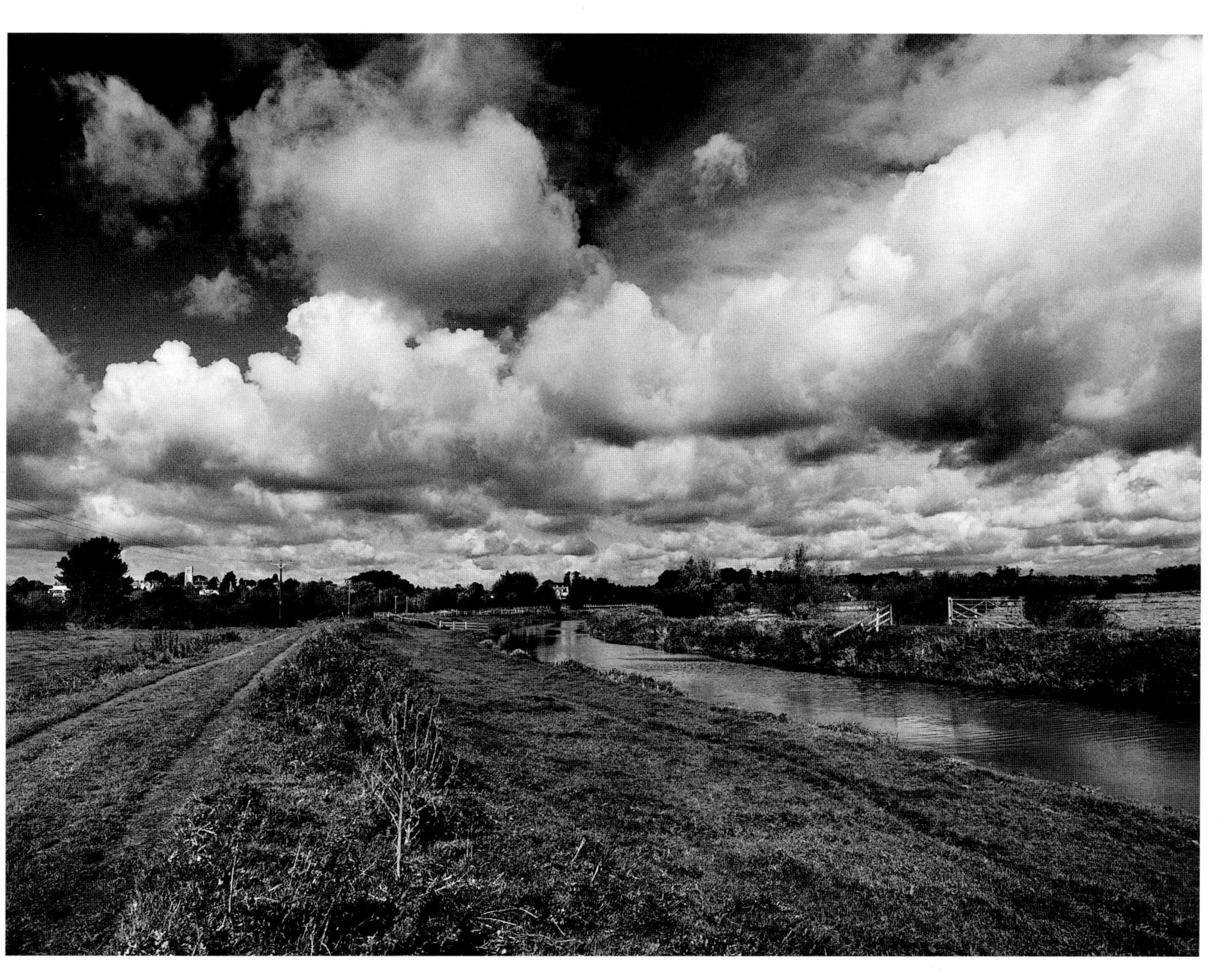

The Parrett Trail, near Langport, Somerset by Michael Mammatt

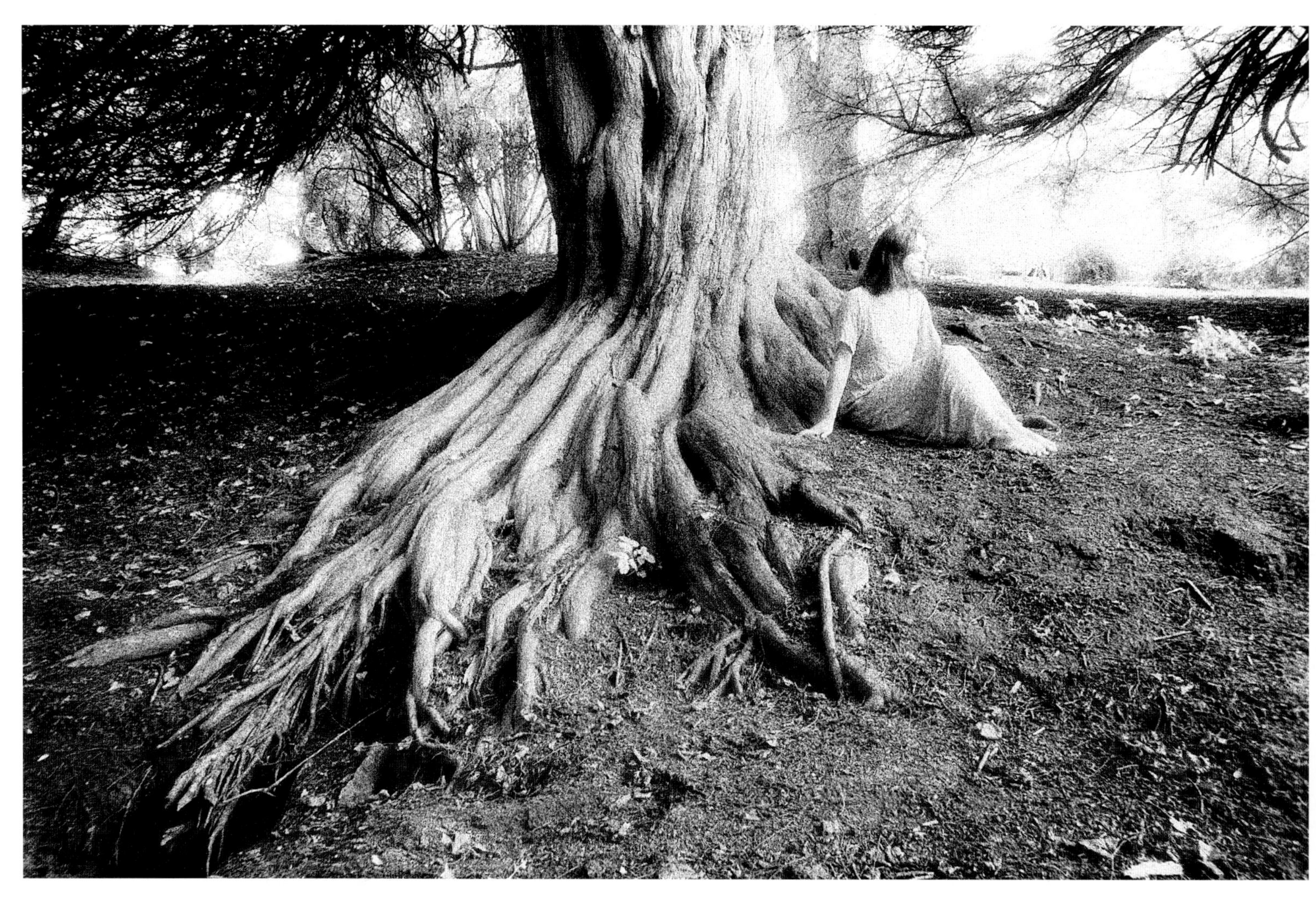

Young Woman in Woodland, Dillington, Somerset by Paul Taylor

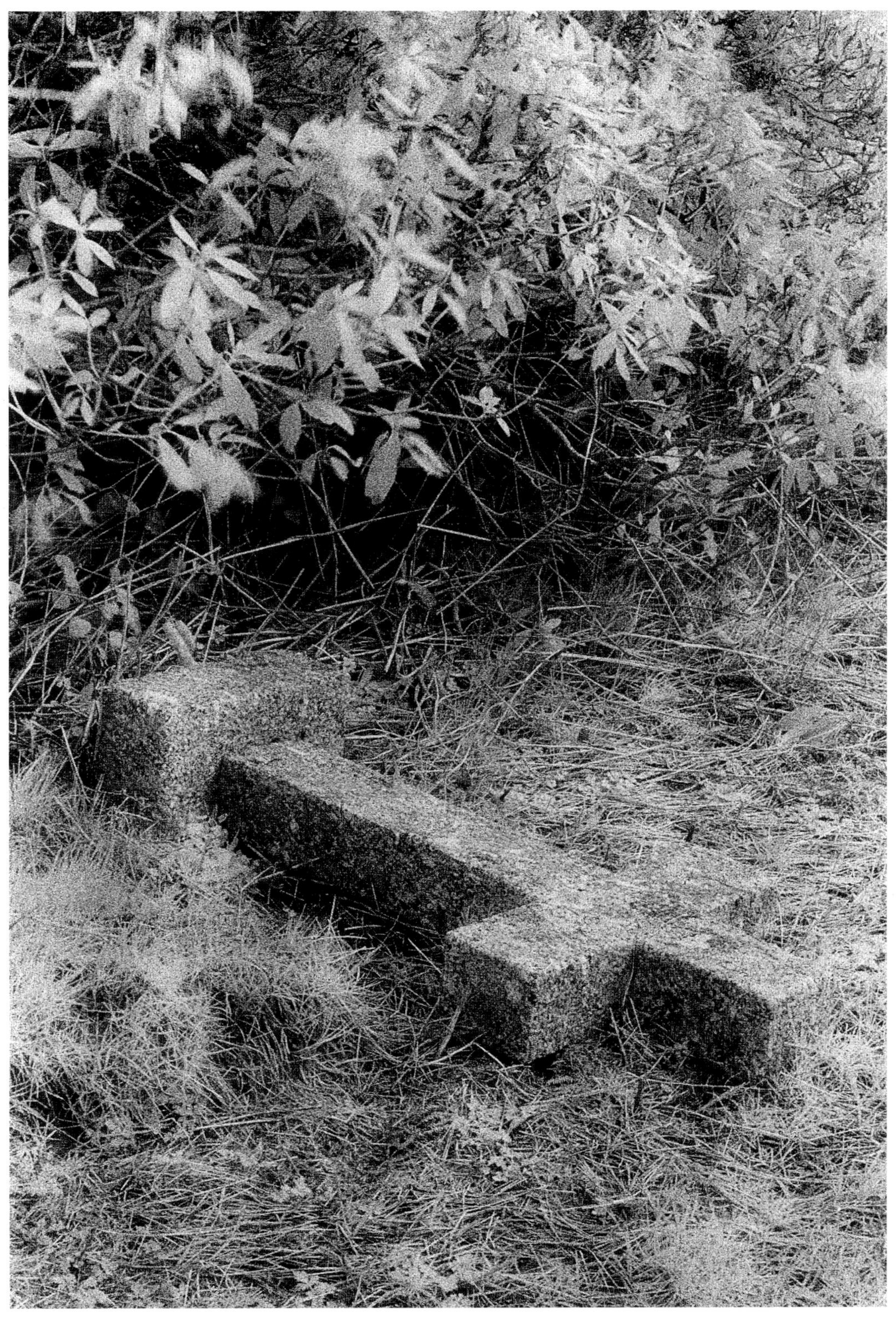

Fallen Cross, Otterford, Somerset by Abbey Thresher

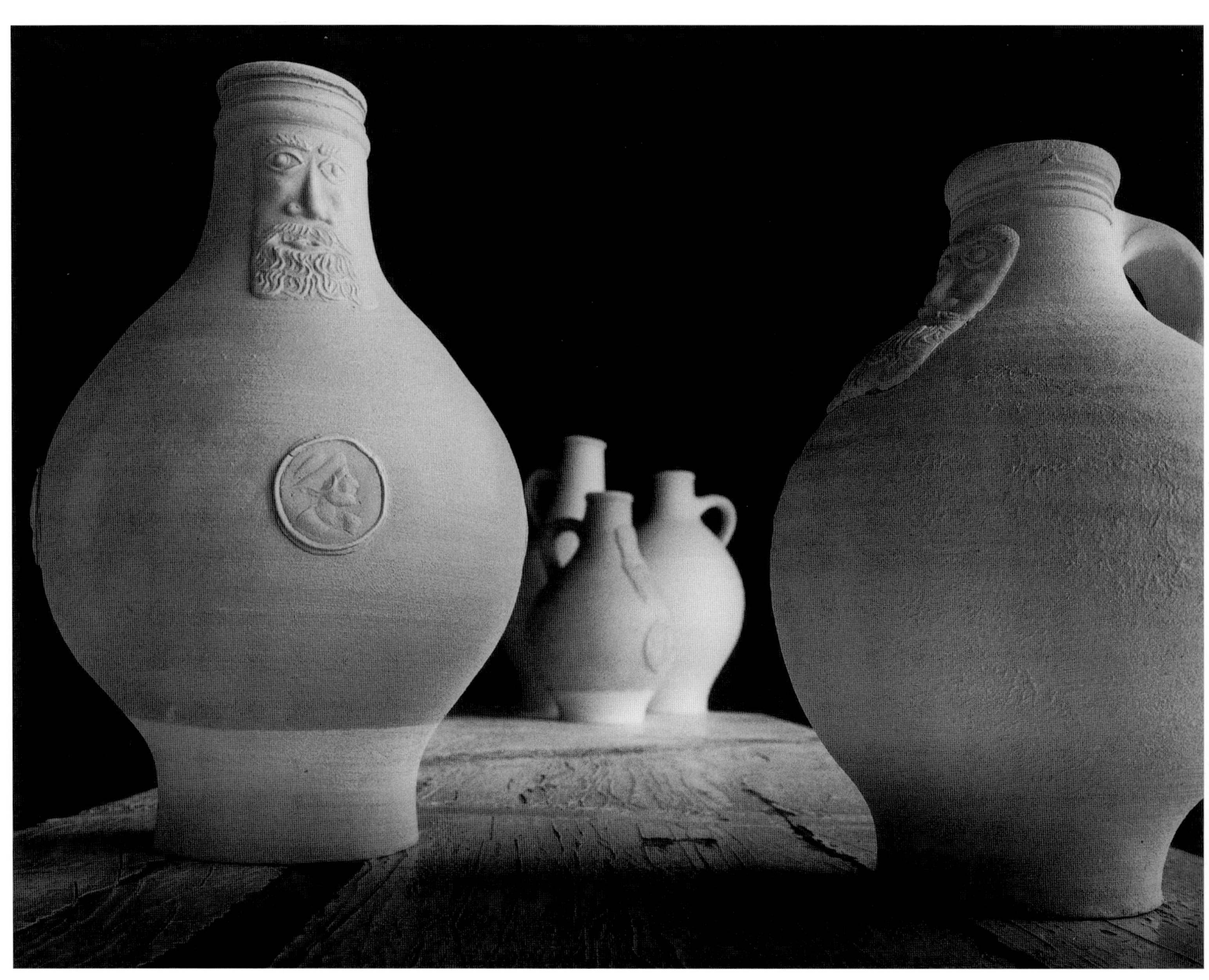

Belarmines, Devon by Keith Smith

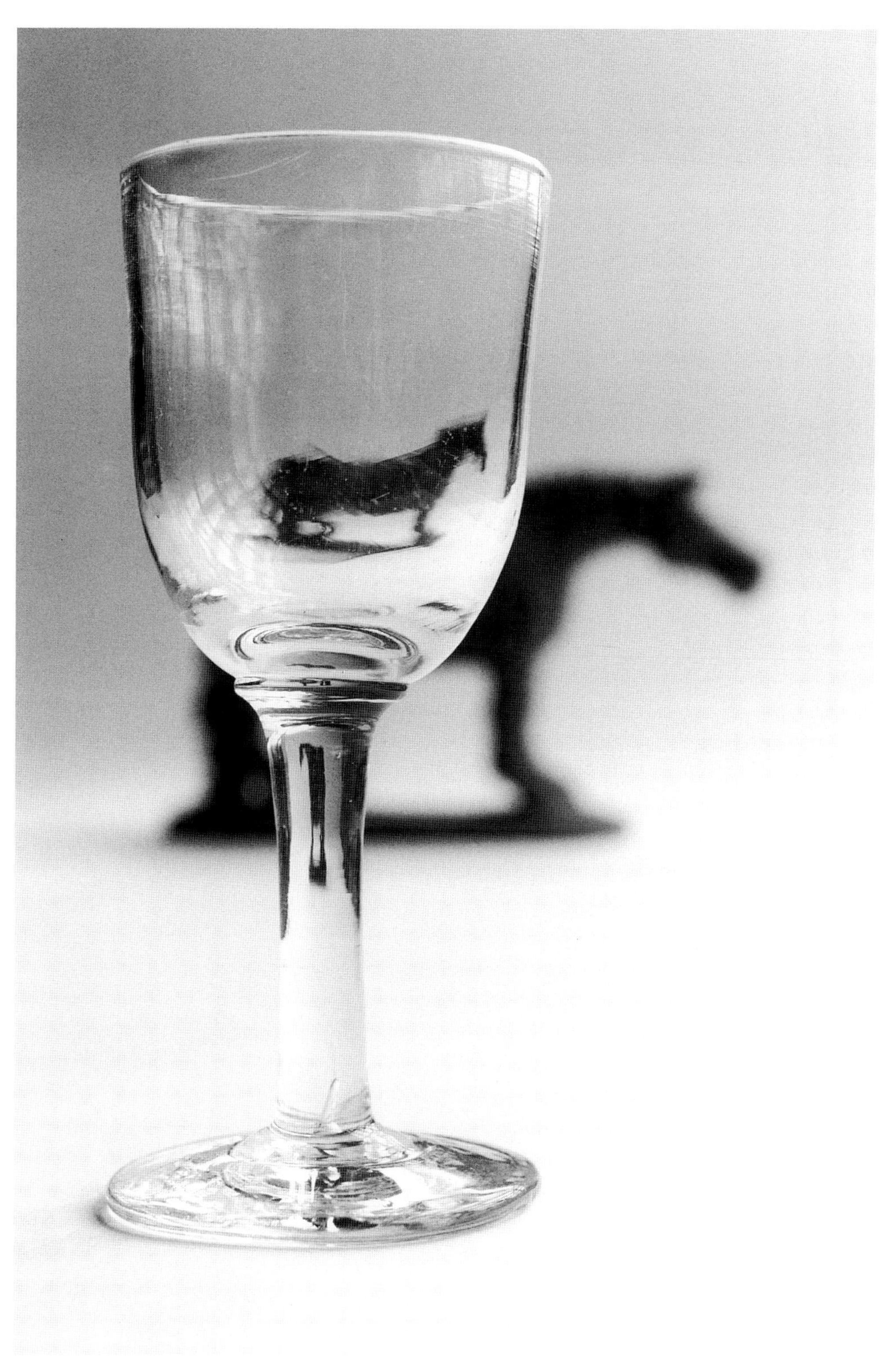

The Photographer's Wineglass, Devon by Keith Smith

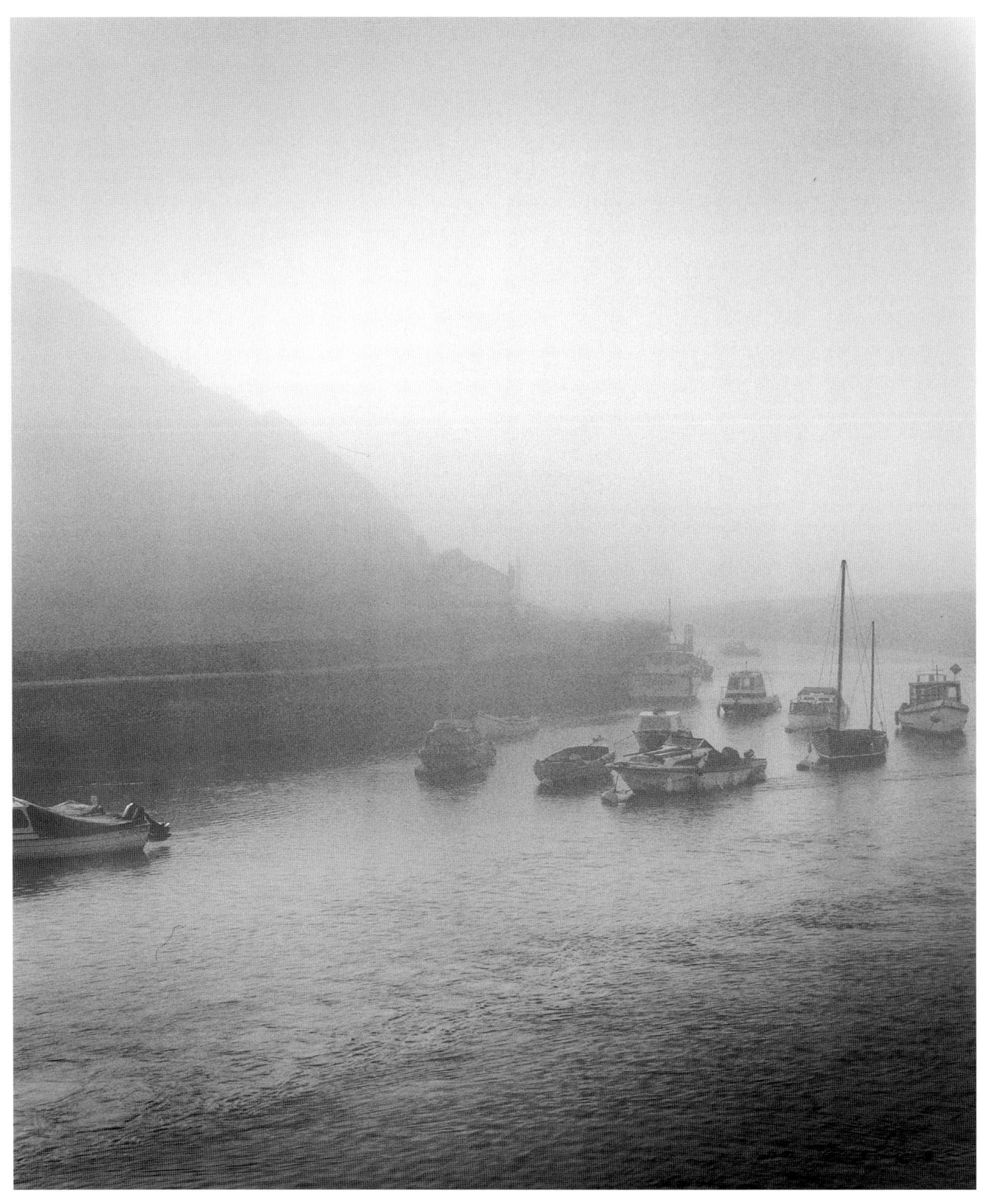

Axmouth Harbour, Devon by Keith Smith

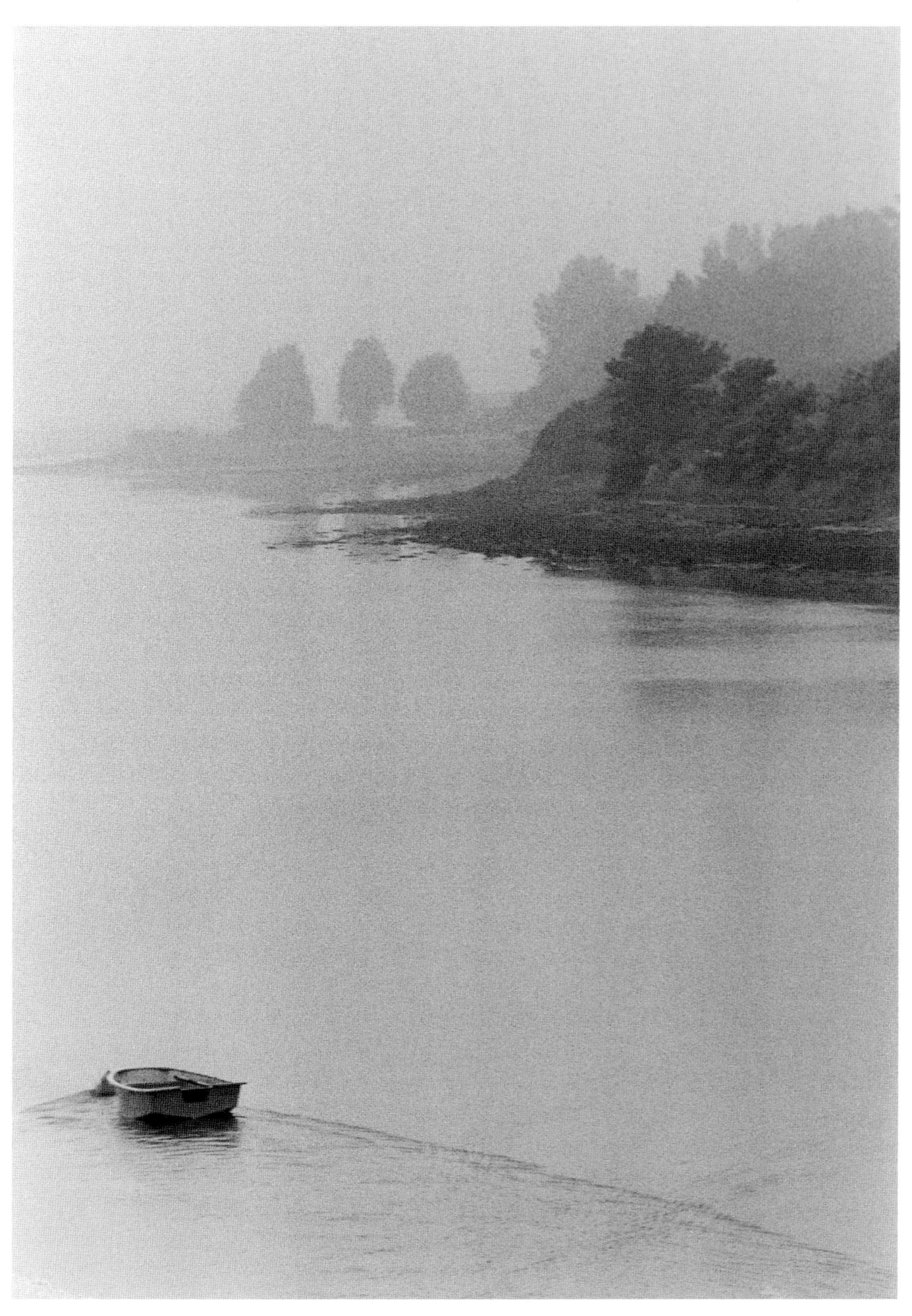

The Axe Estuary, Devon by Keith Smith

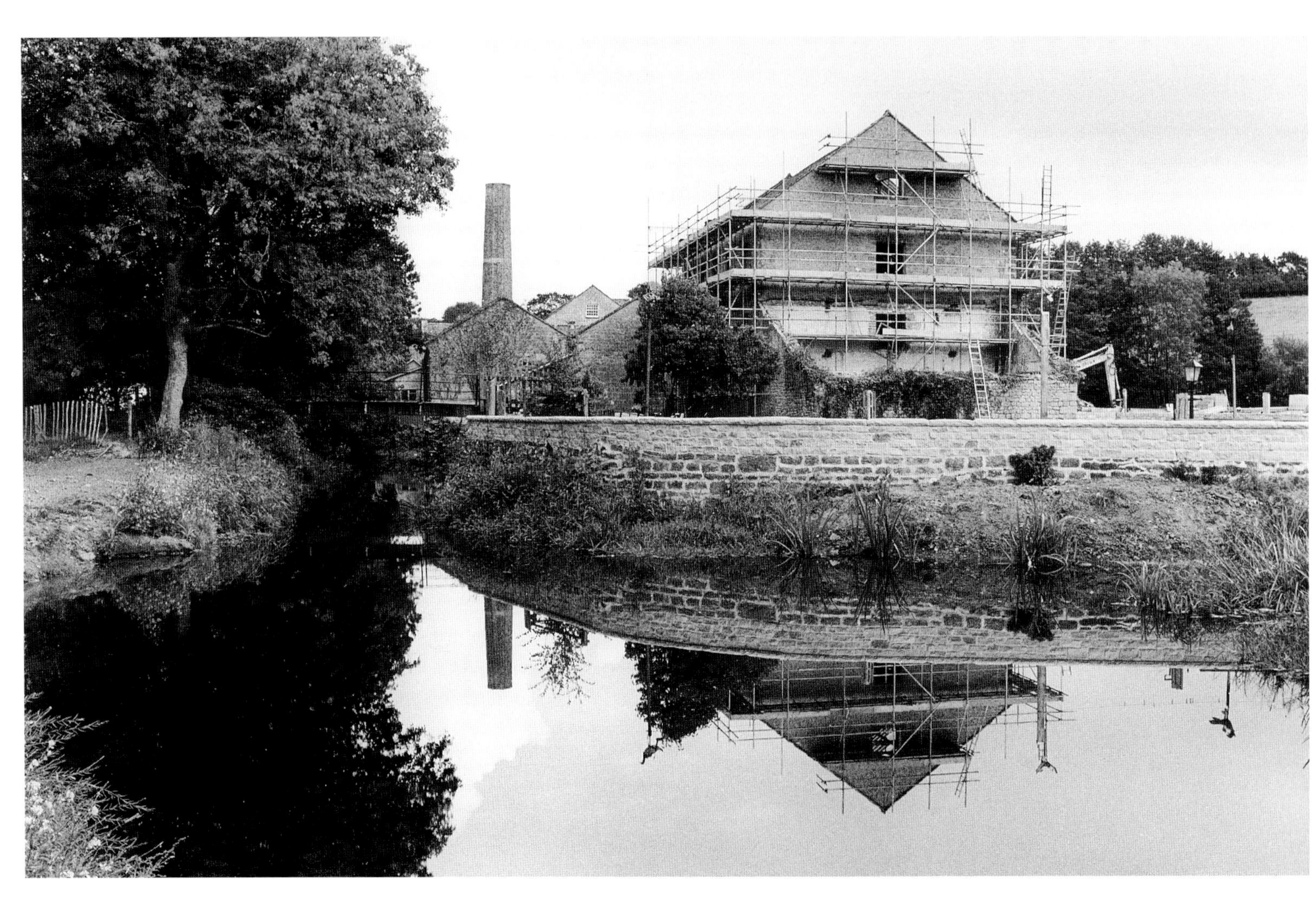

The Rebirth of Old Pymore, Dorset by Dianne Dowling

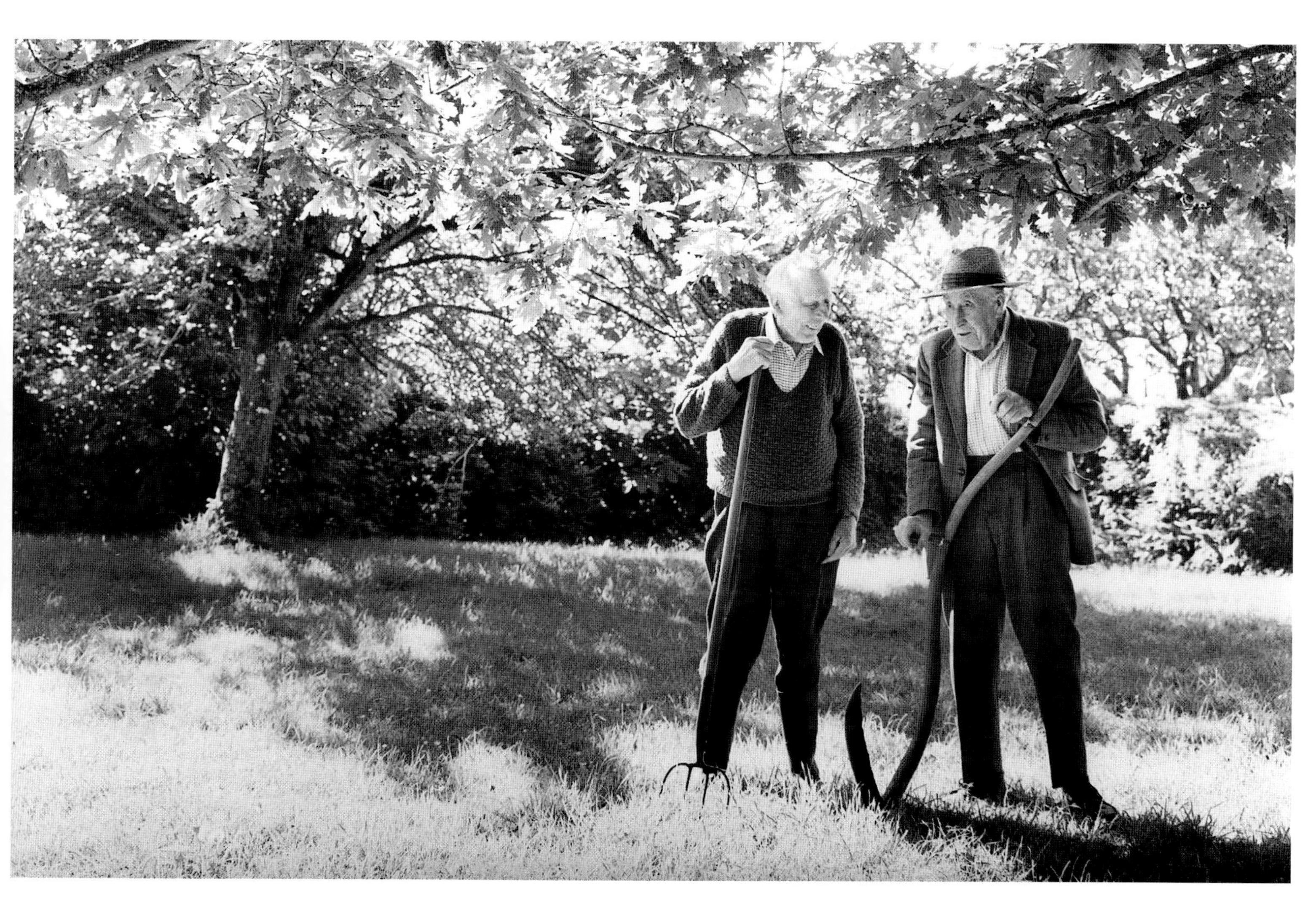

Jack and Jim Webber, aged 97 and 99, Jobbing Gardeners, Stoke Abbott, Dorset by Pauline Rook

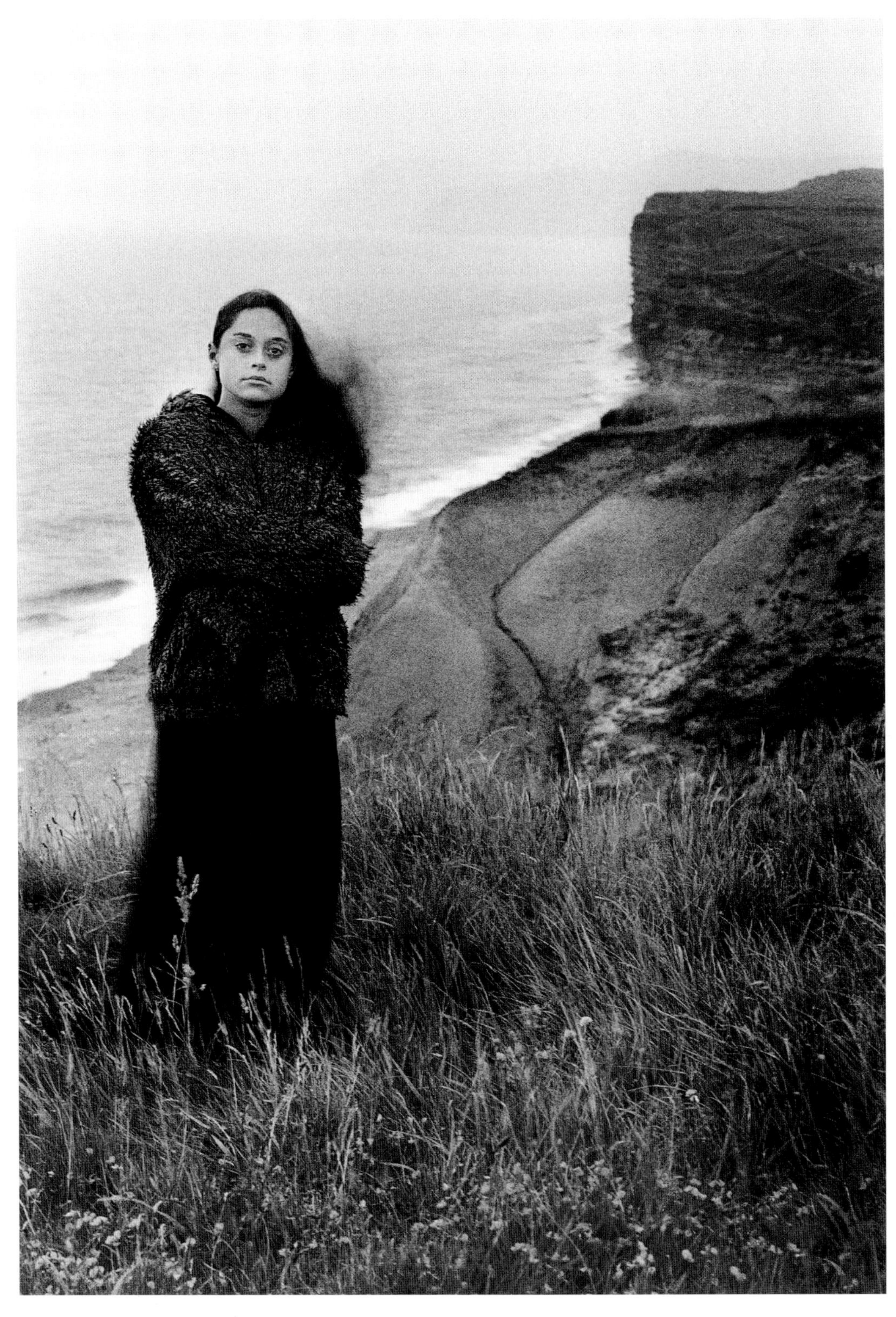

Miriam, East Cliff, Burton Bradstock, Dorset by Pat Garth

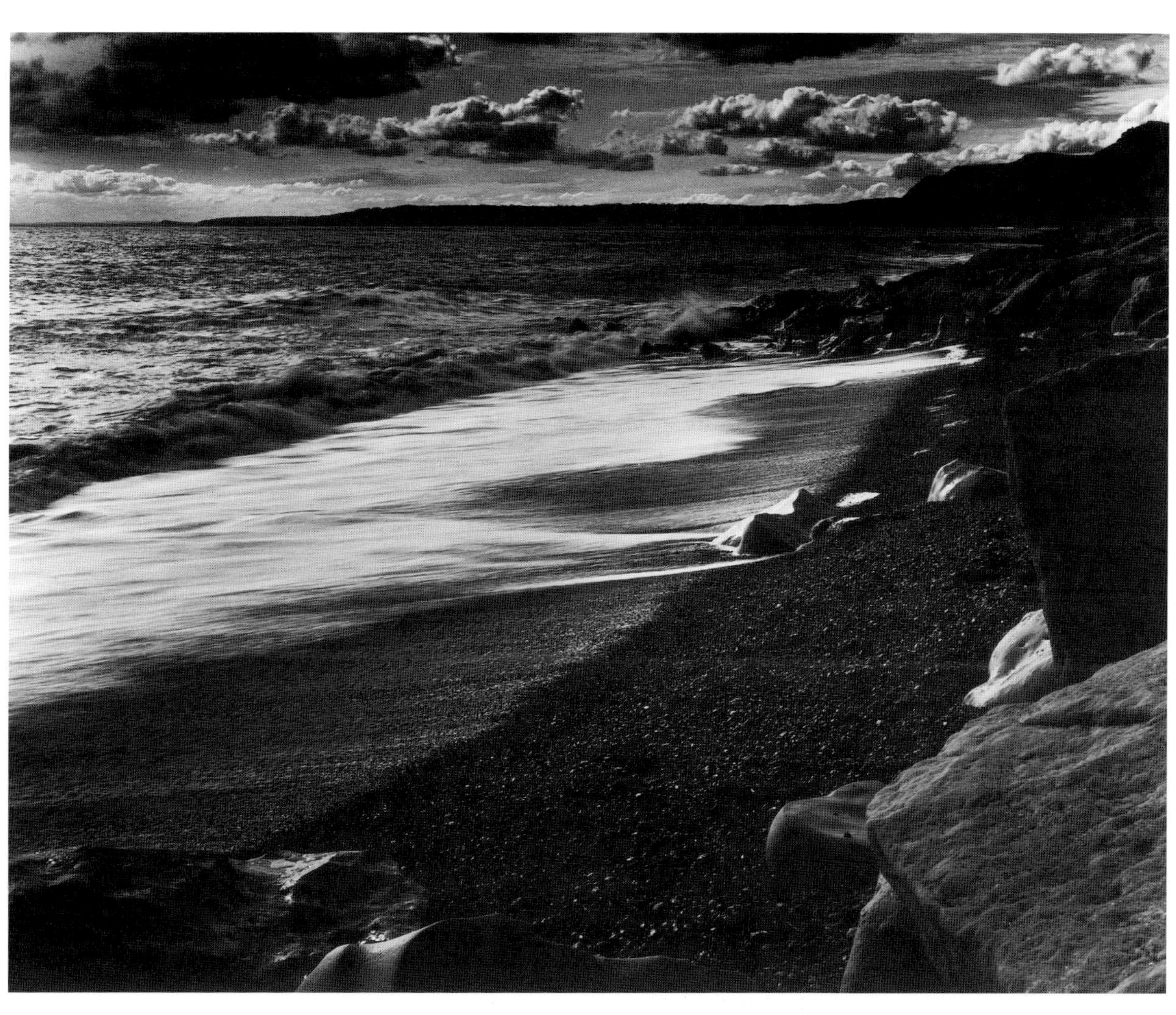

West Bay, Dorset by Emma Weal

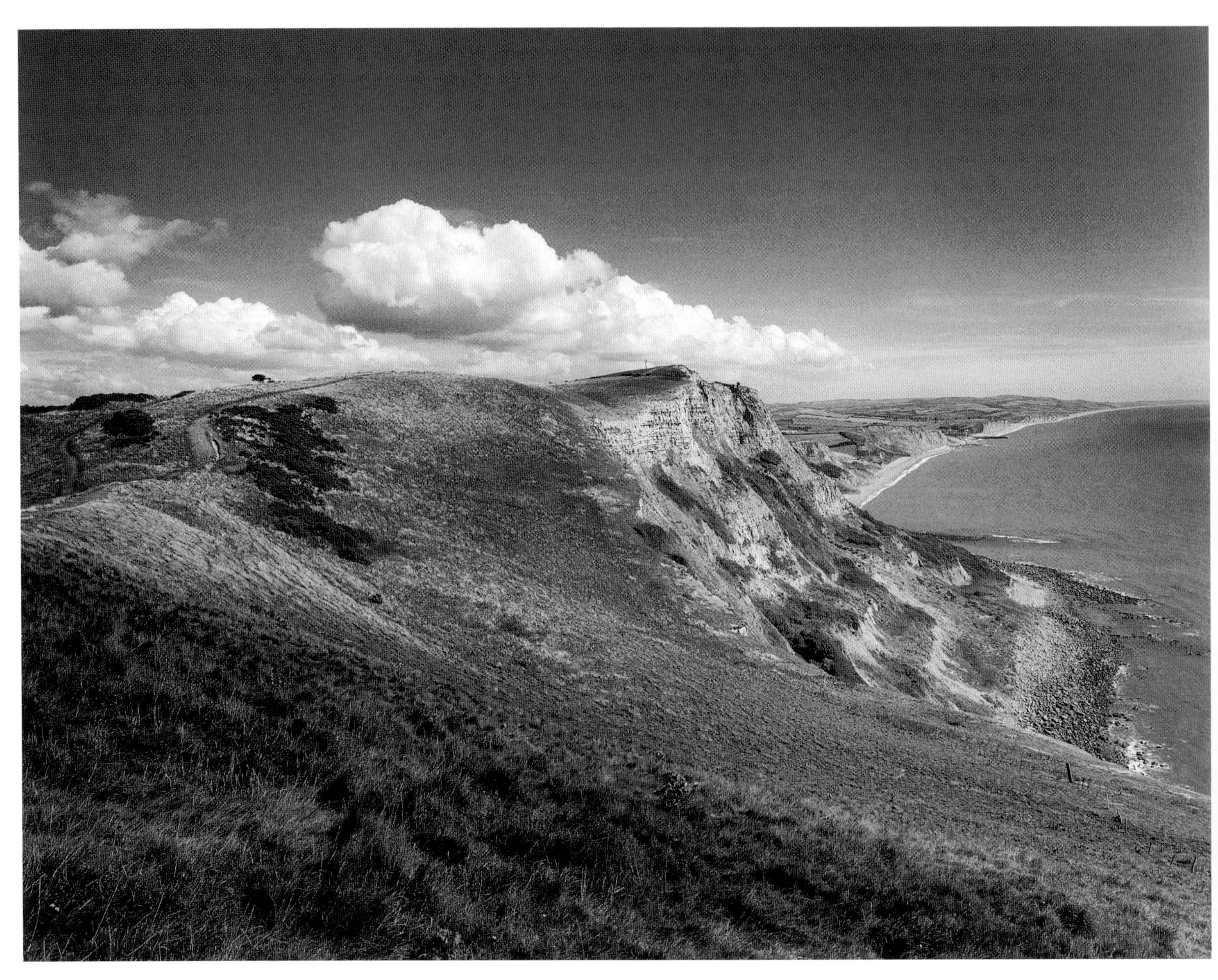

West Bay from Thorncombe Beacon, Dorset by Ulick Palmer

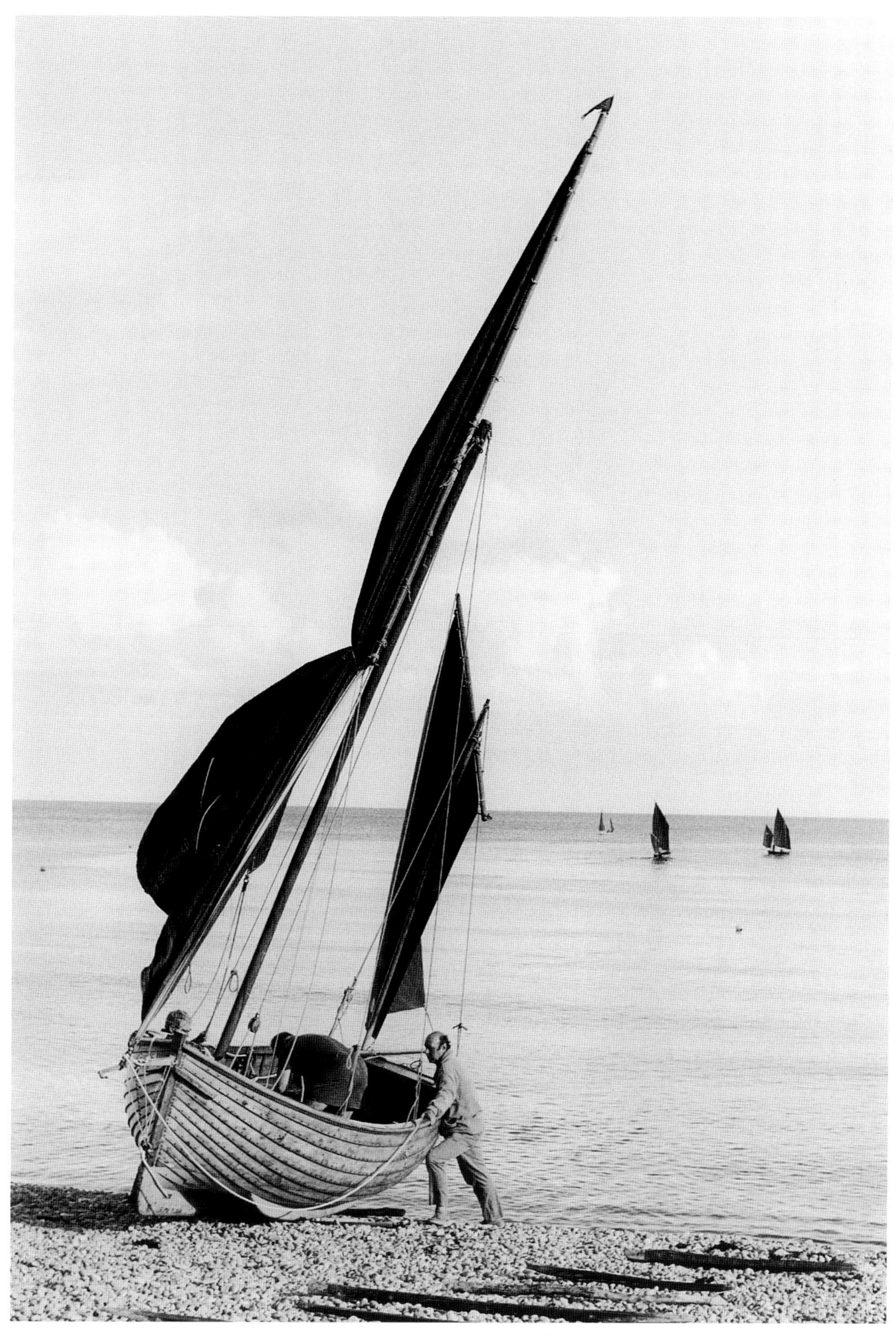

Beer Luggers, Beer, Devon by Carol Green

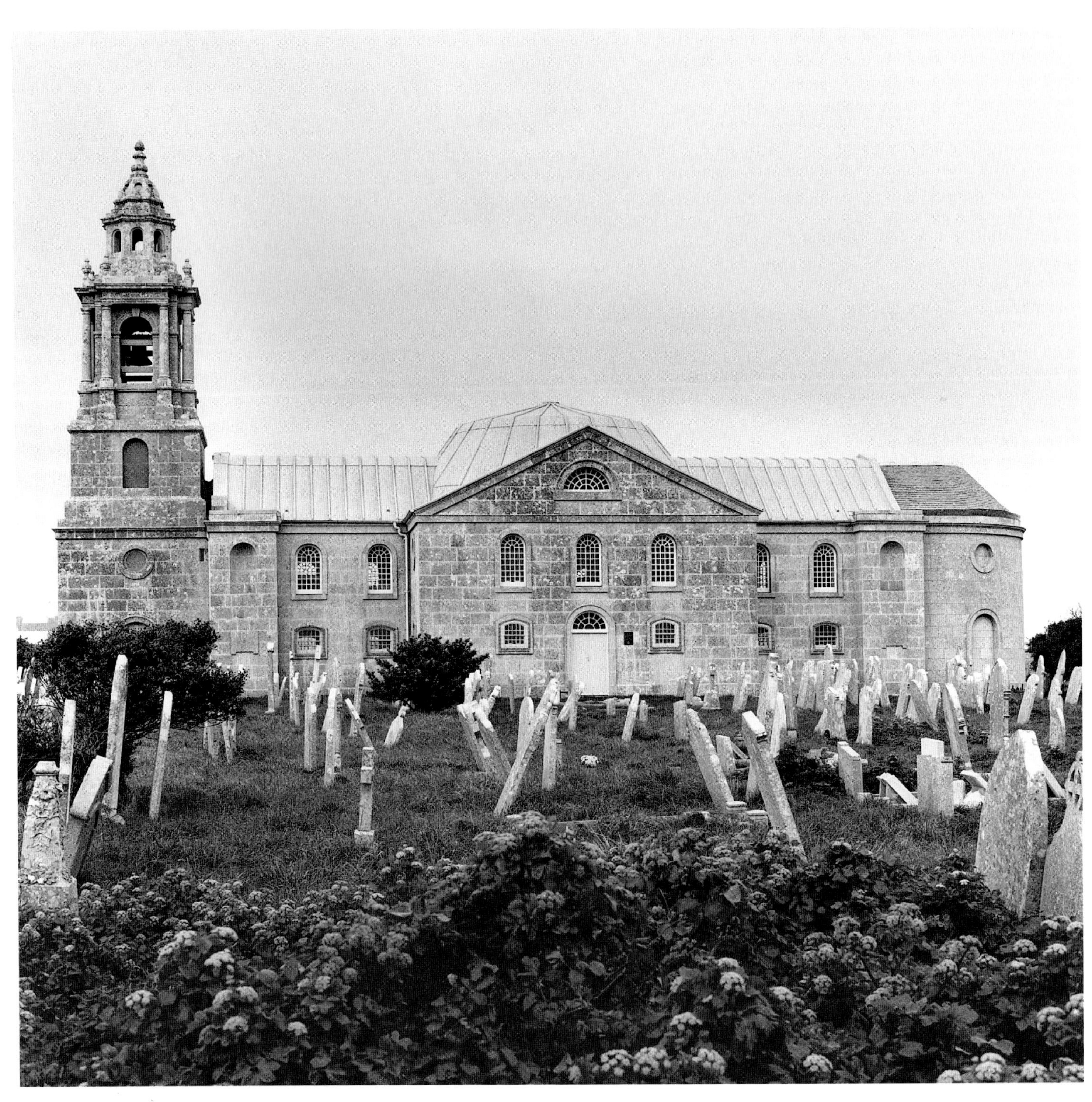

St. George's Church, Reforne, Isle of Portland, Dorset by Robin Mills

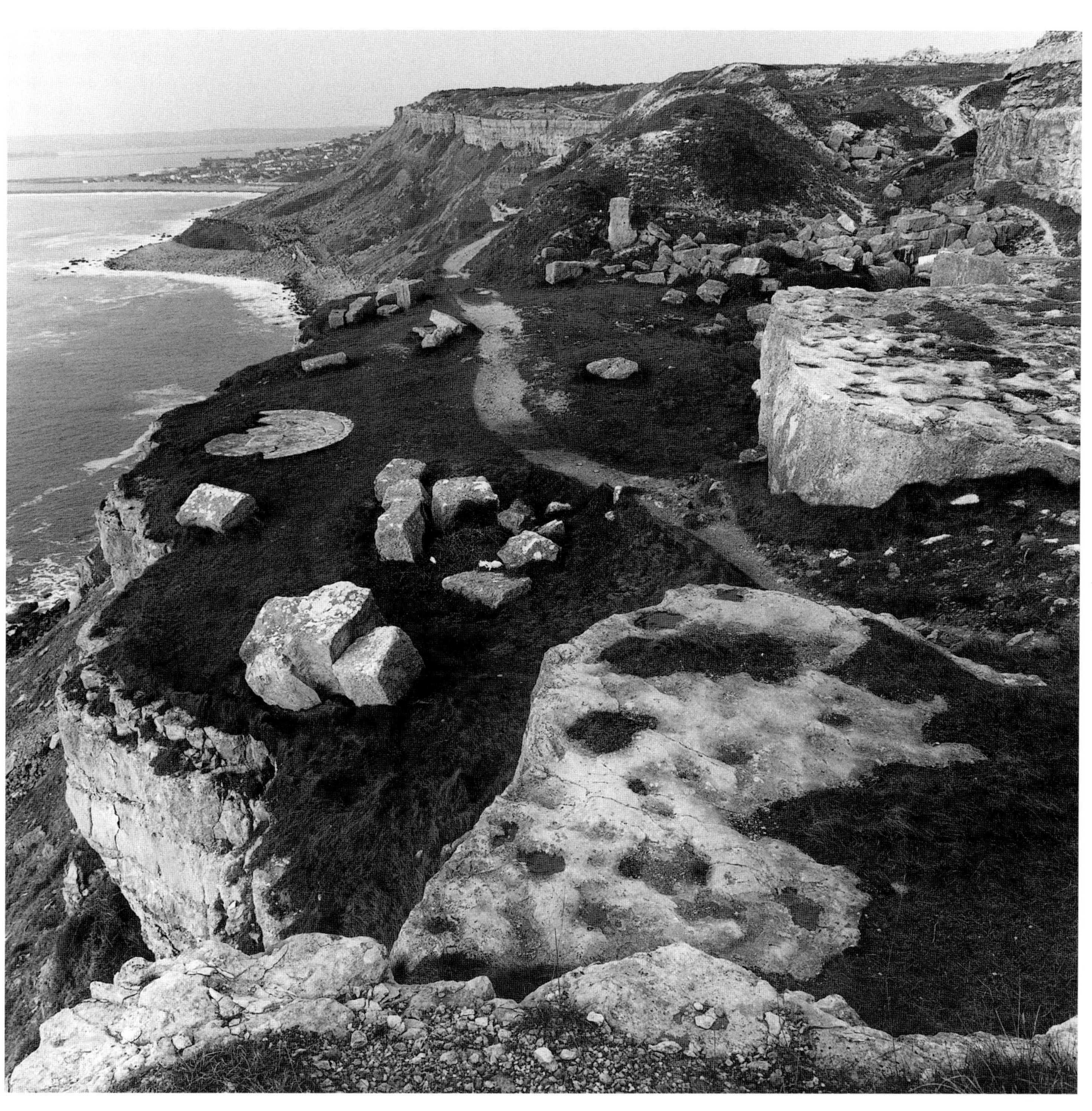

West Cliffs, Isle of Portland, Dorset by Robin Mills

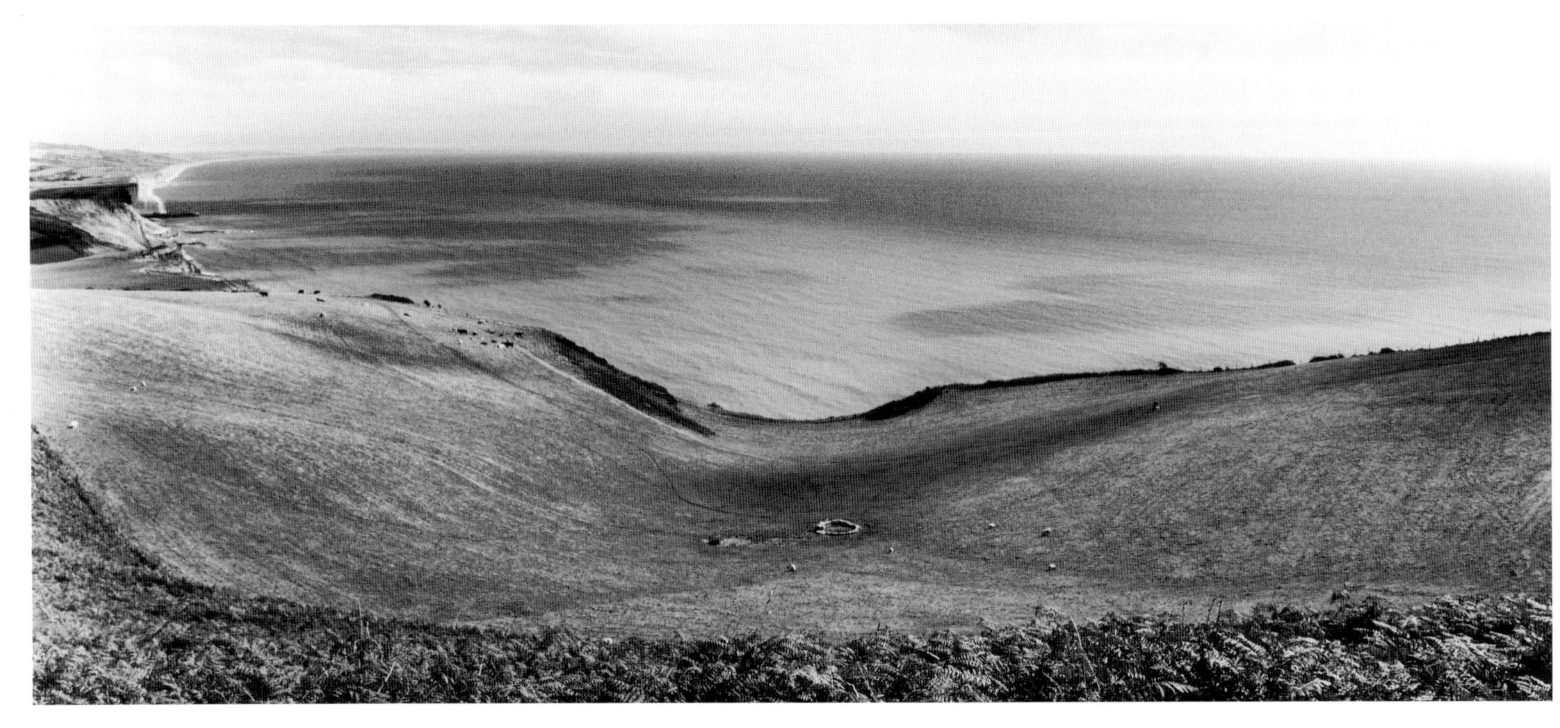

Coastal Meadow from Thorncombe Beacon, Dorset by Brian Smyth

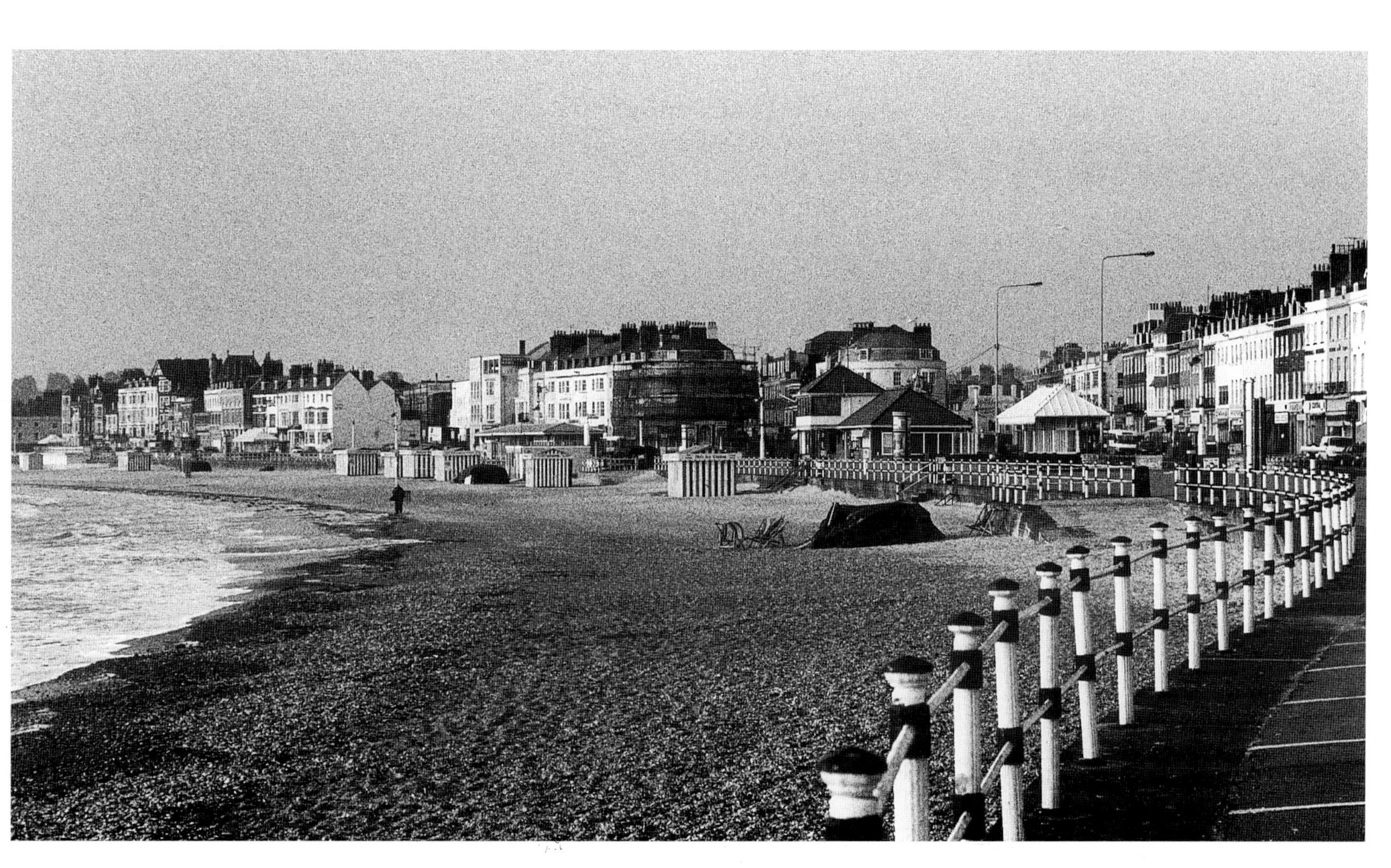

Seafront, Weymouth, Dorset by Kirsten Cooke

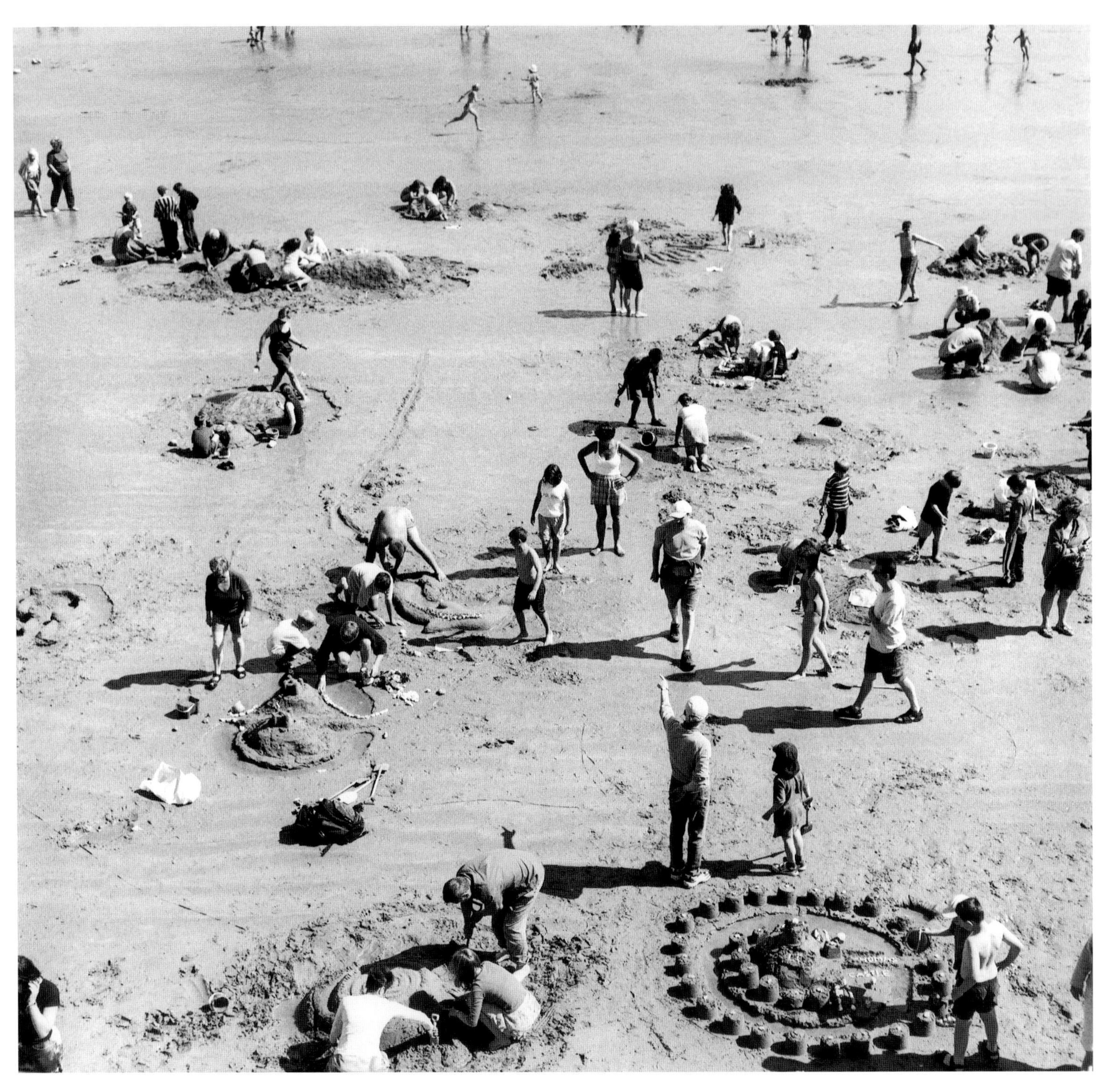

People on the Beach, Lyme Regis, Dorset by Maisie Hill

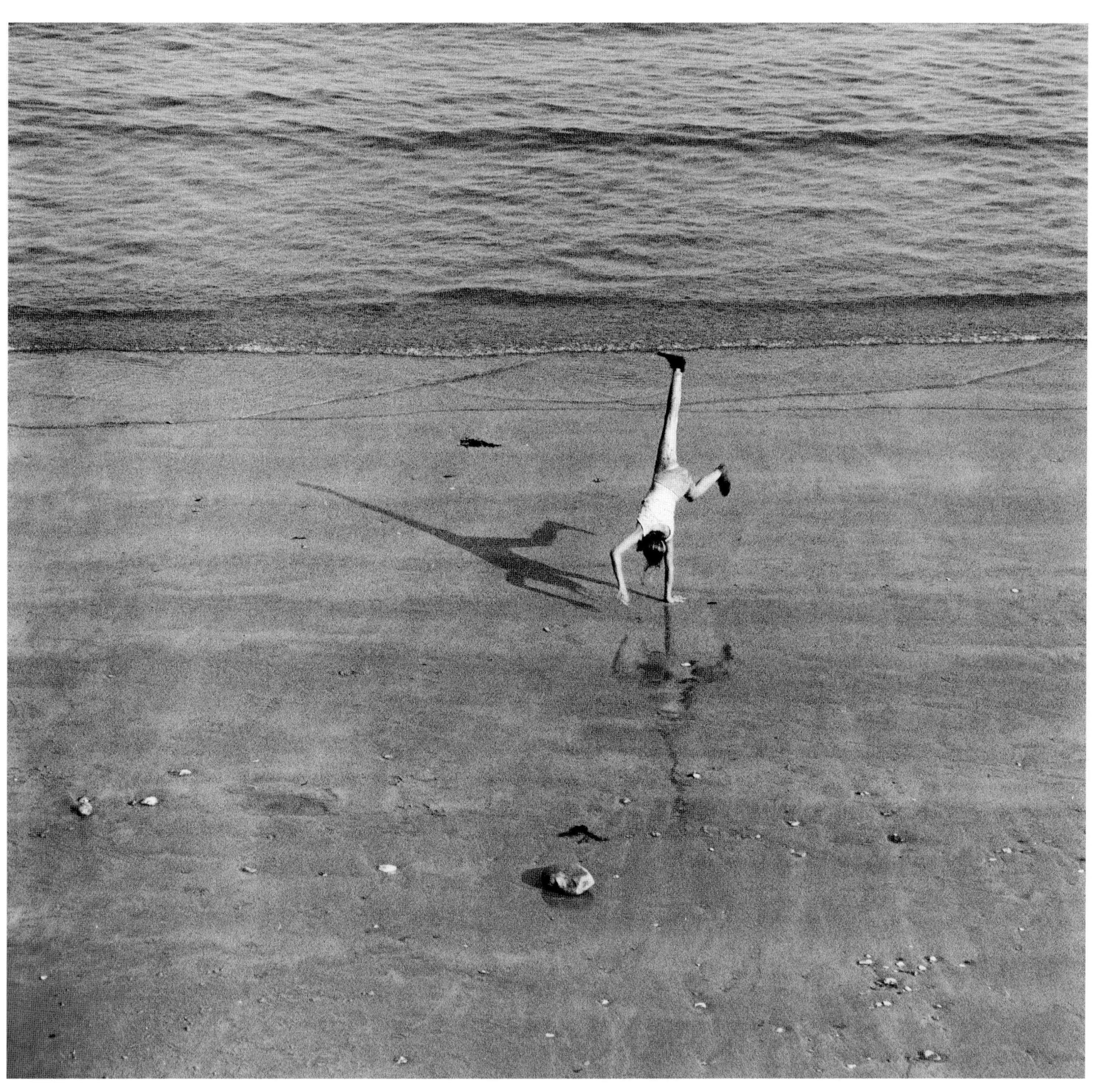

Cartwheel, Lyme Regis, Dorset by Maisie Hill

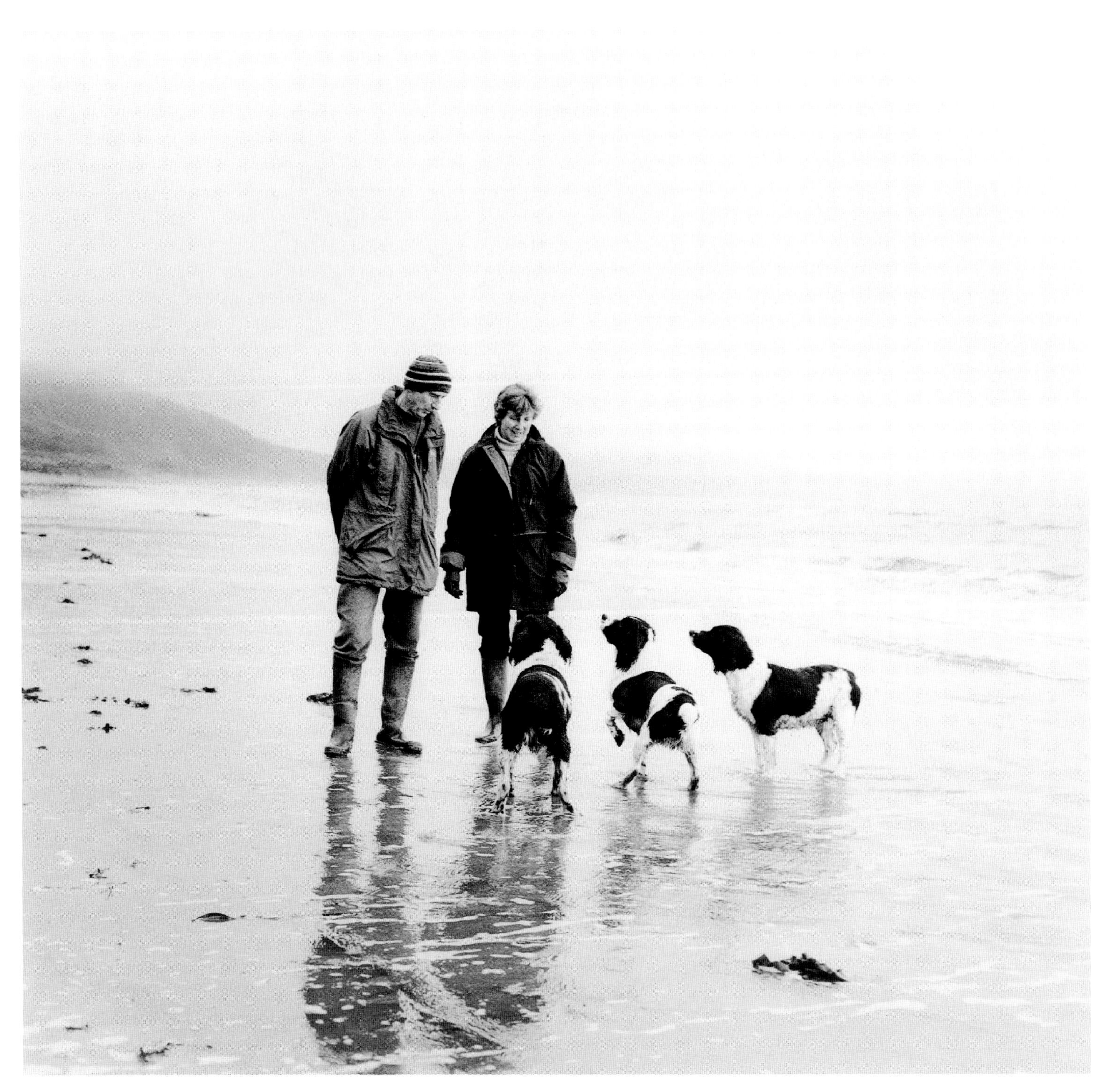

Spaniels, Lyme Regis, Dorset by Maisie Hill

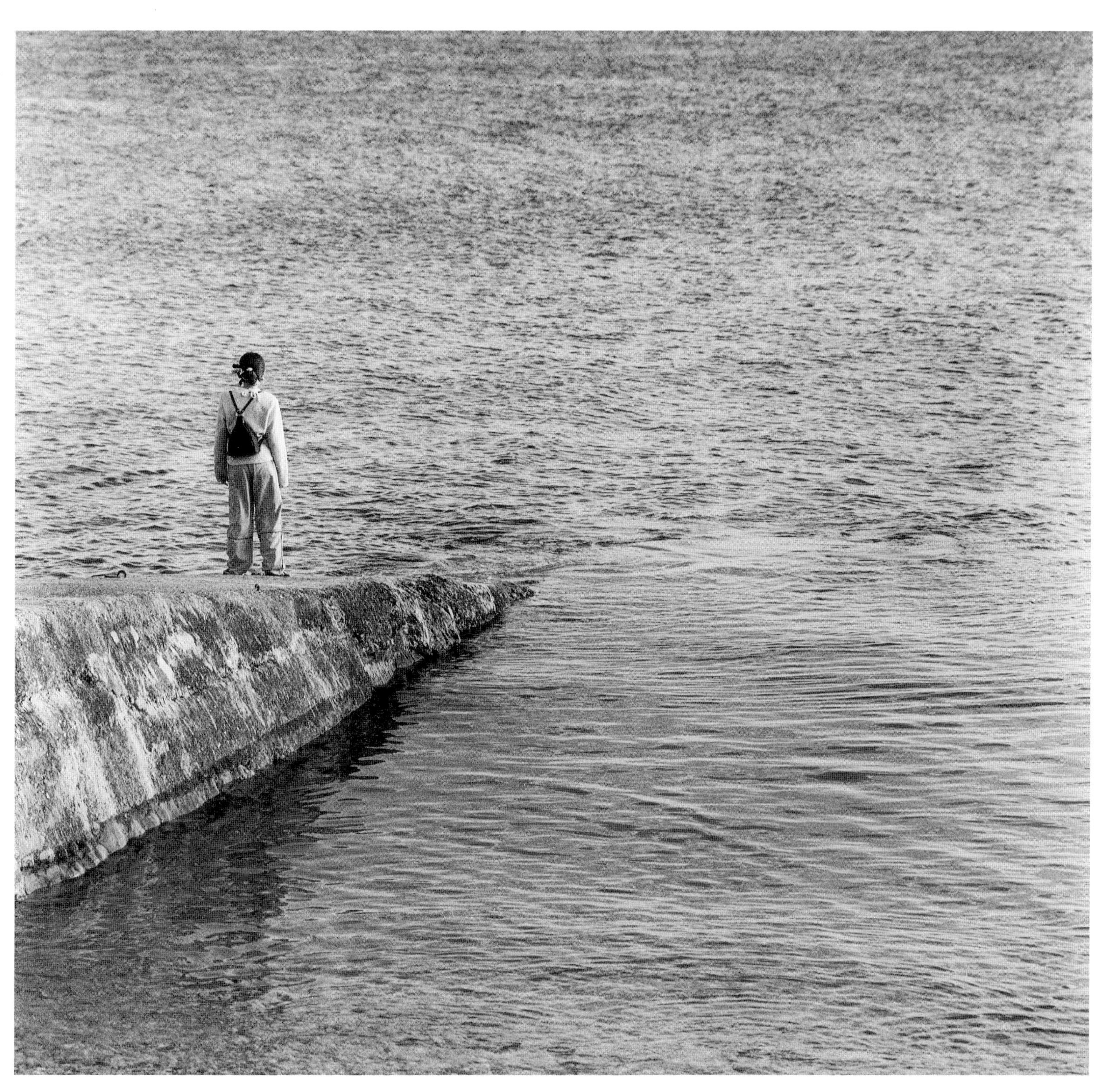

Woman on Jetty, Lyme Regis, Dorset by Maisie Hill

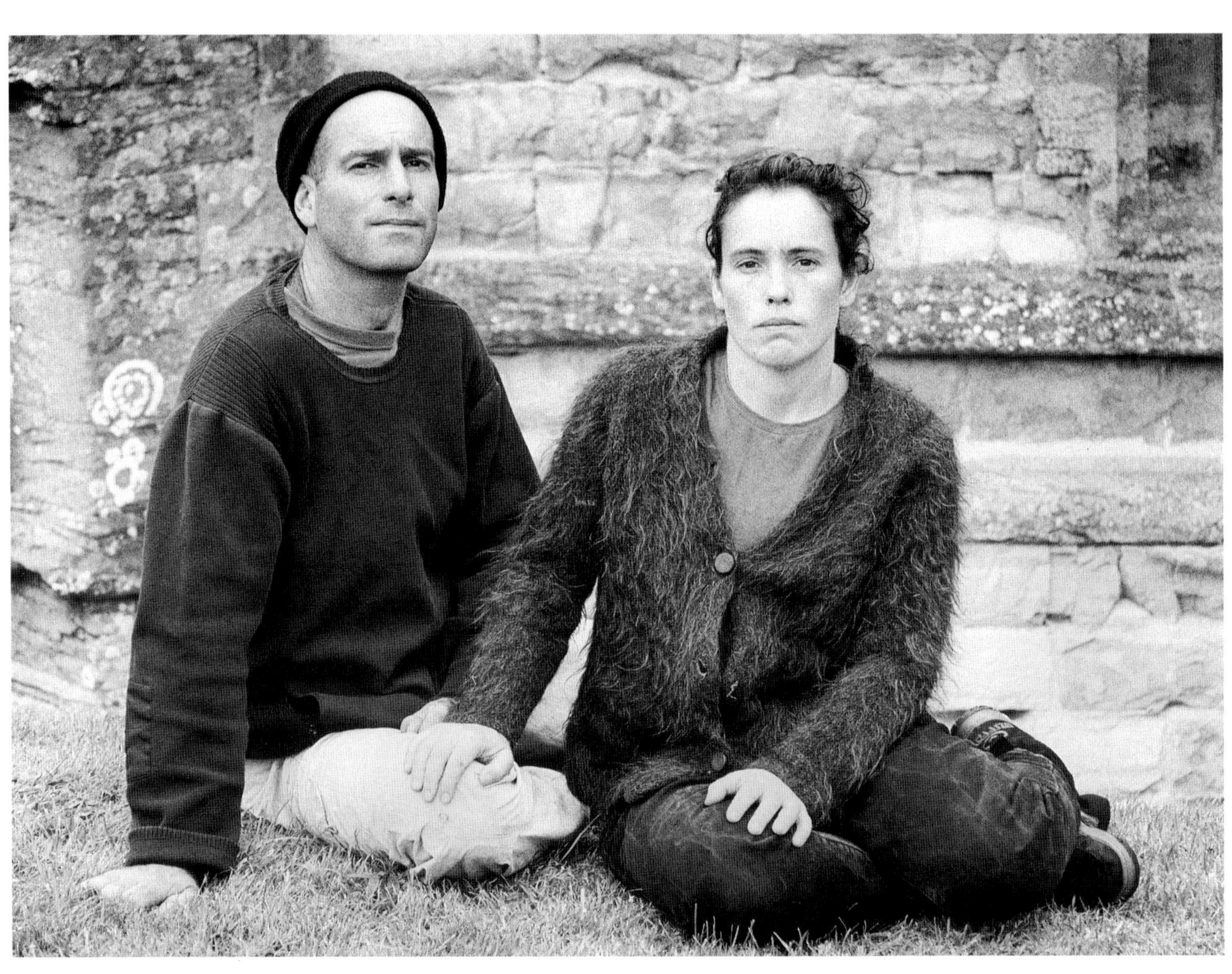

Maisie and Kevin, Lyme Regis, Dorset by Adrian Turton

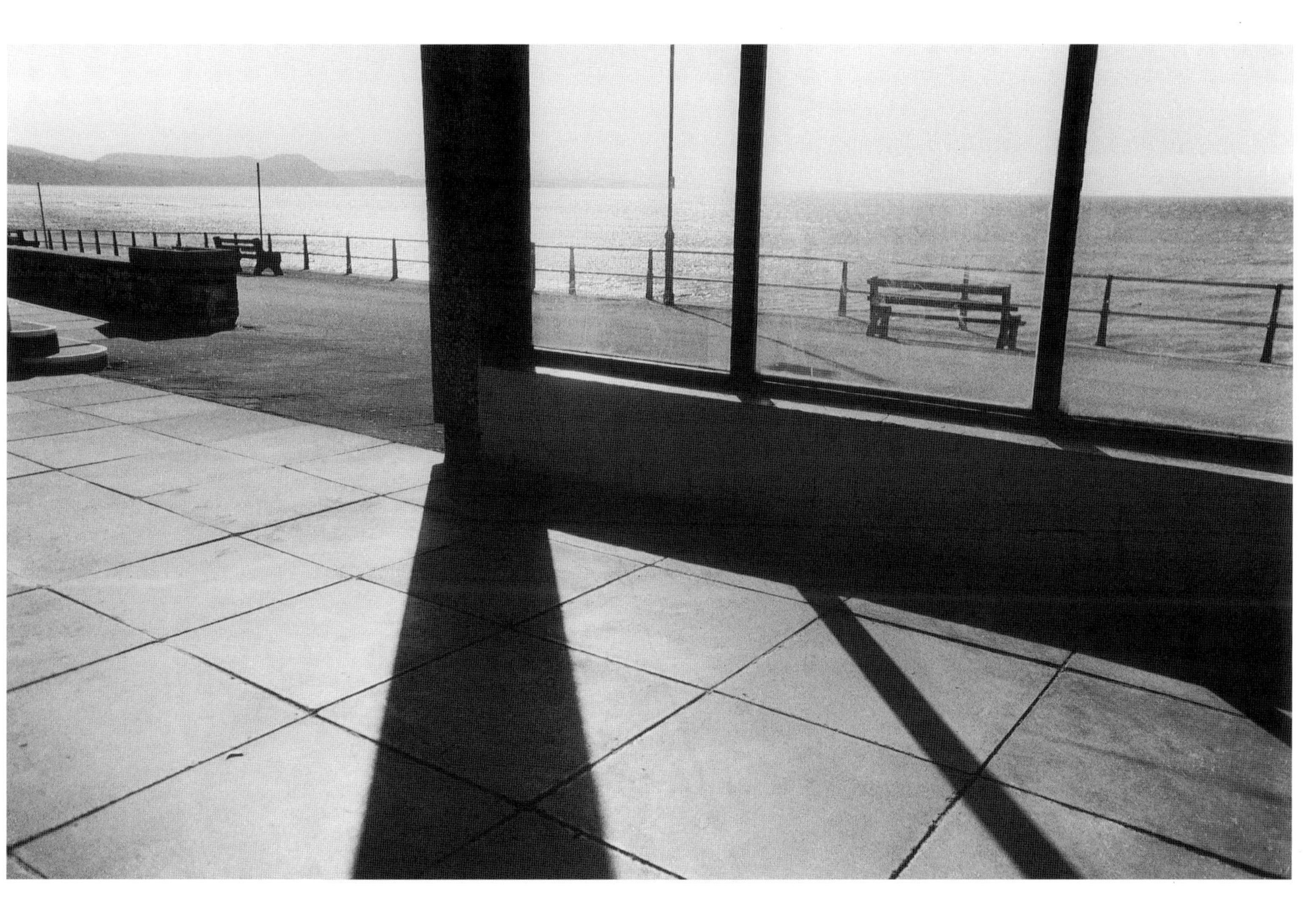

Lyme Regis, Dorset by Katia Marsh

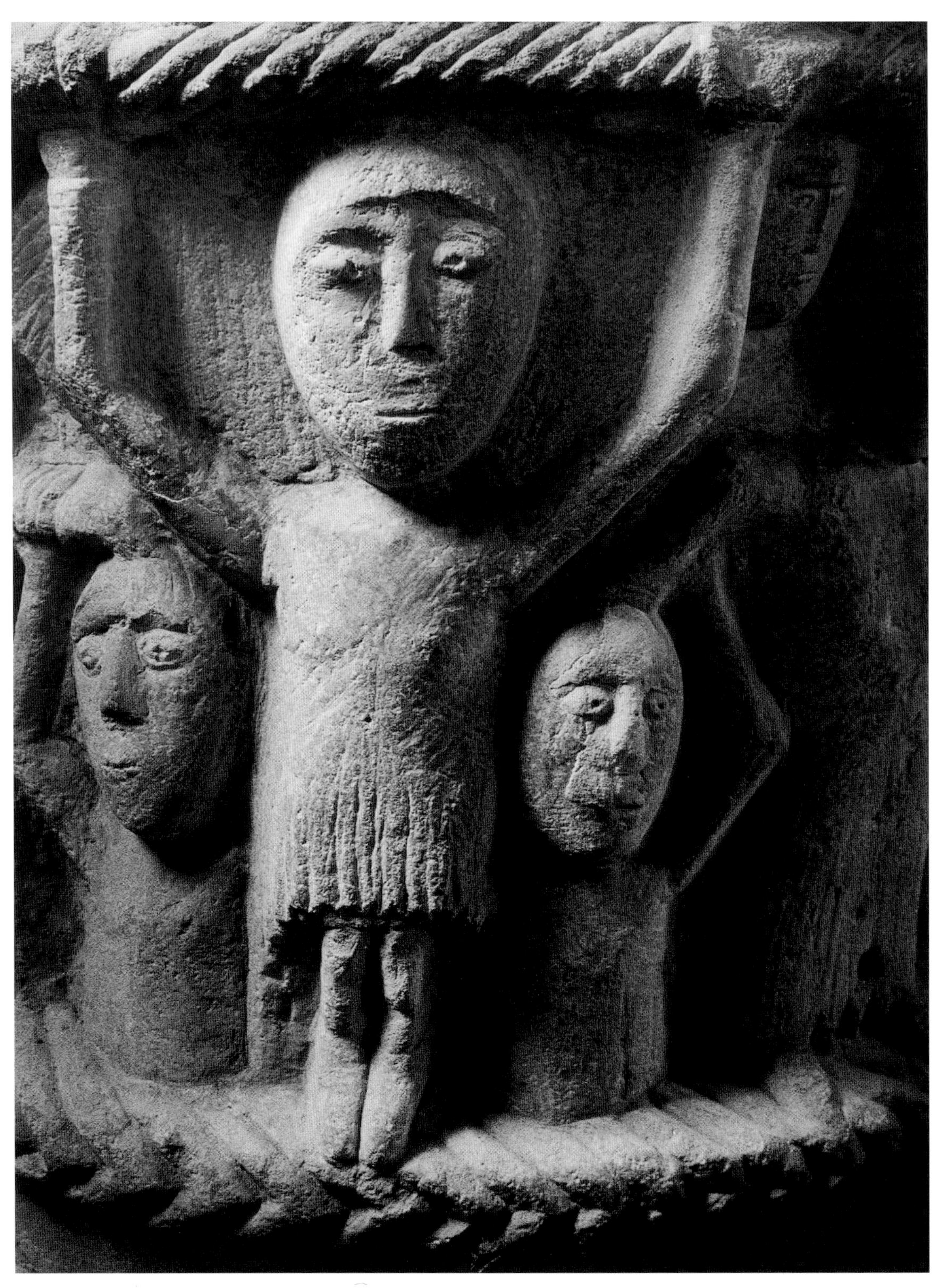

Font, Toller Fratrum, Dorset by Janet Carmichael

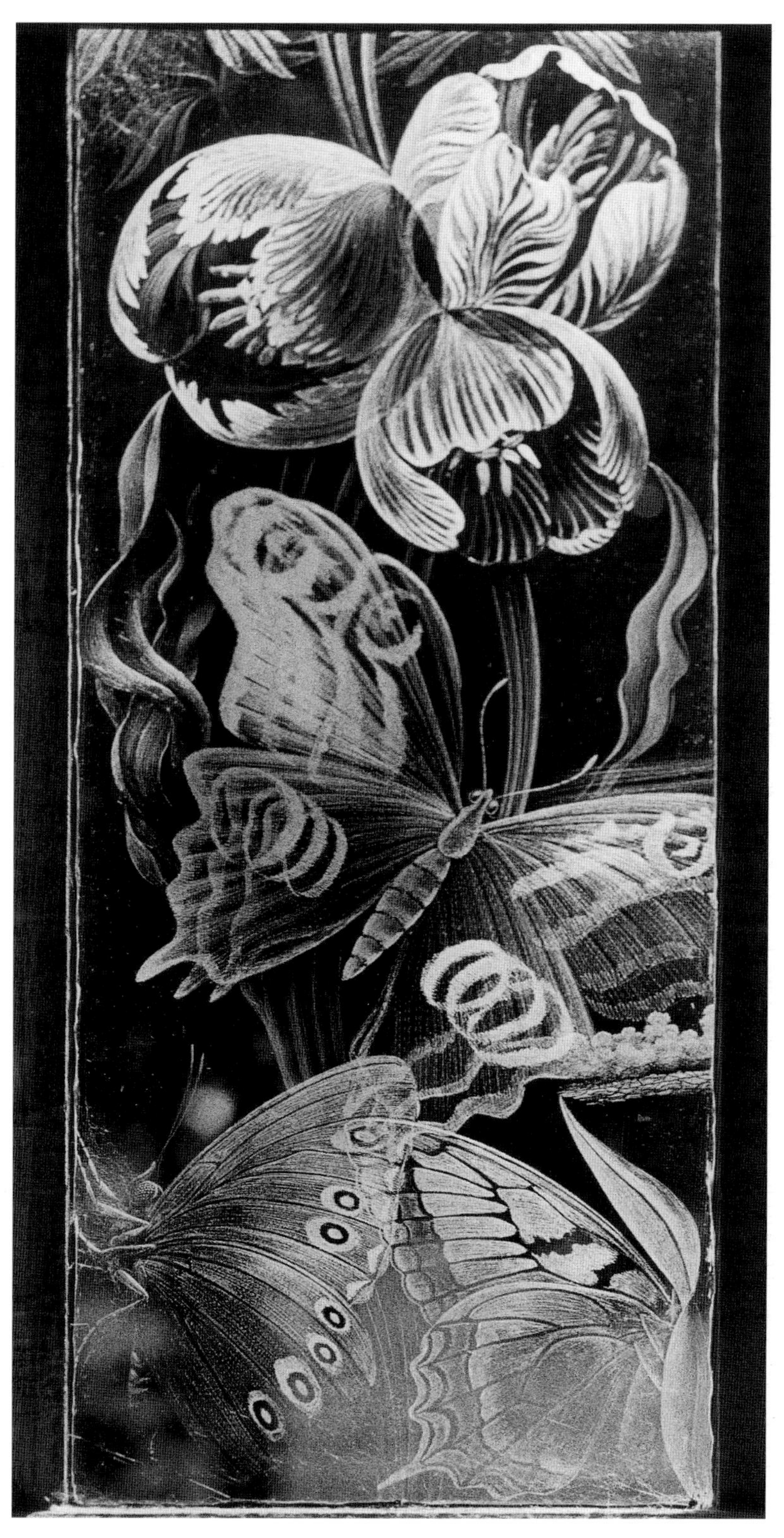

Whistler Etched Glass, St. Nicholas, Moreton, Dorset by Pat Garth

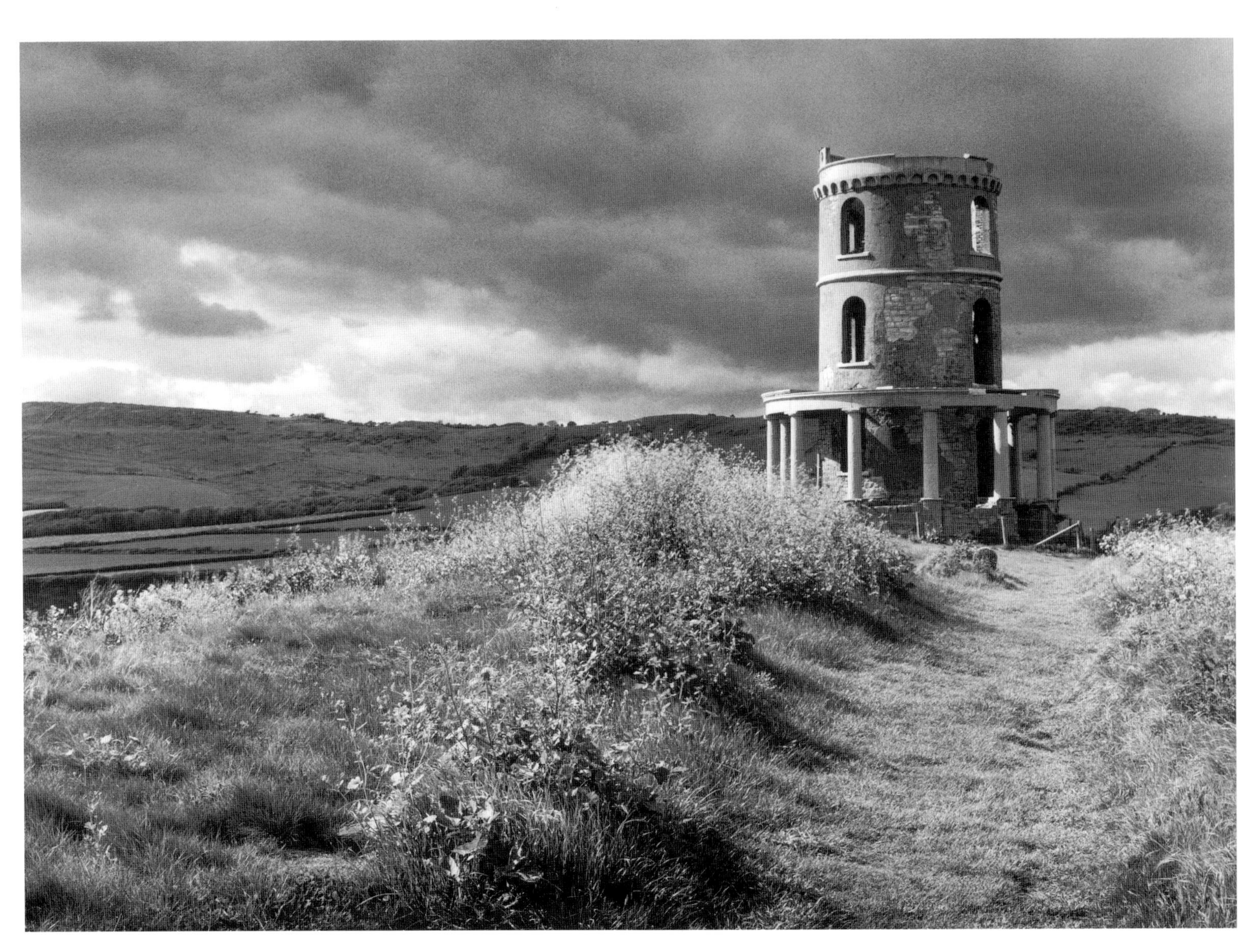

Clavel's Tower, above Kimmeridge Bay, Dorset by Rob Dyson

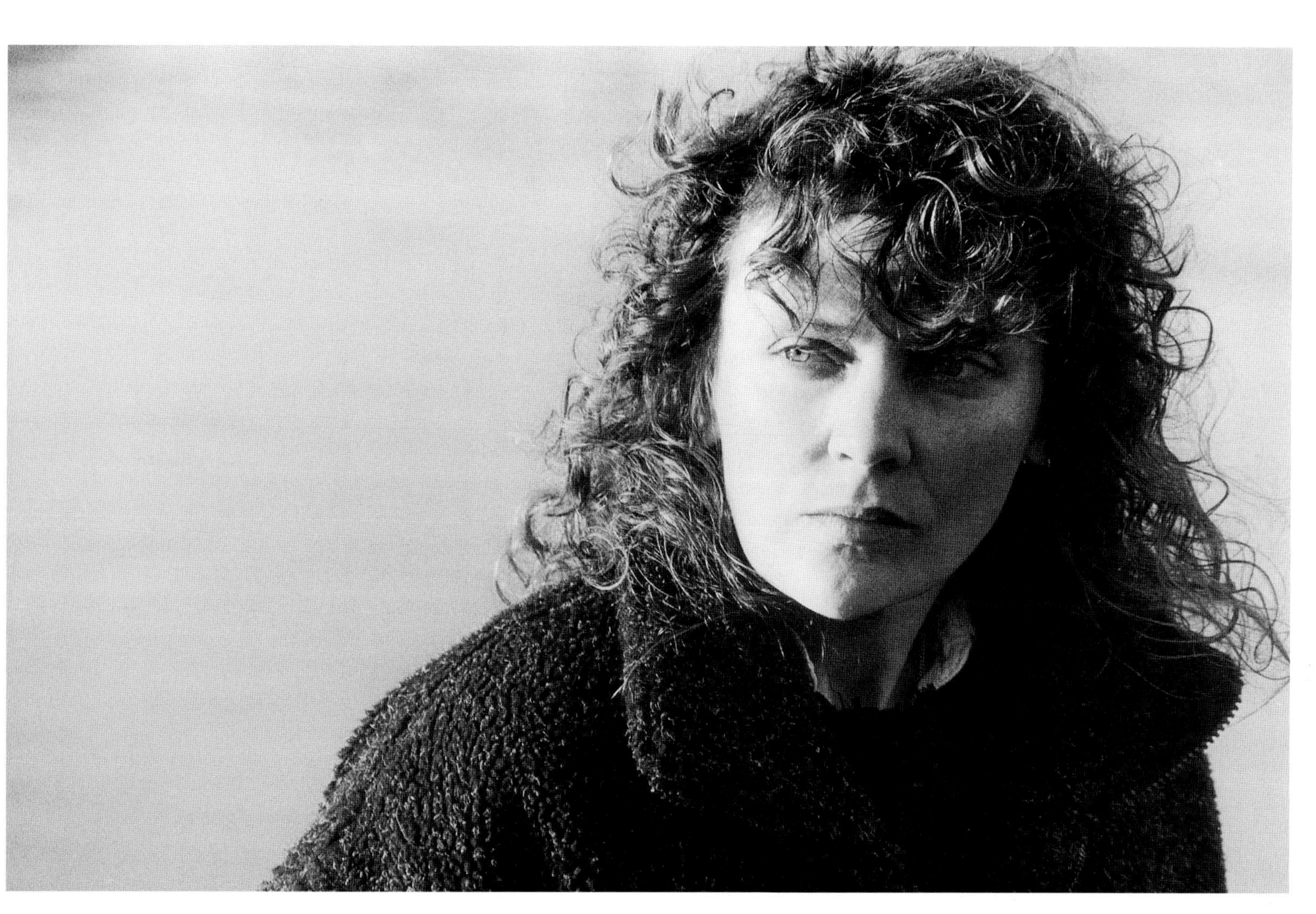

Jennie, Artist and Picture Framer, Lyme Regis, Dorset by Pat Garth

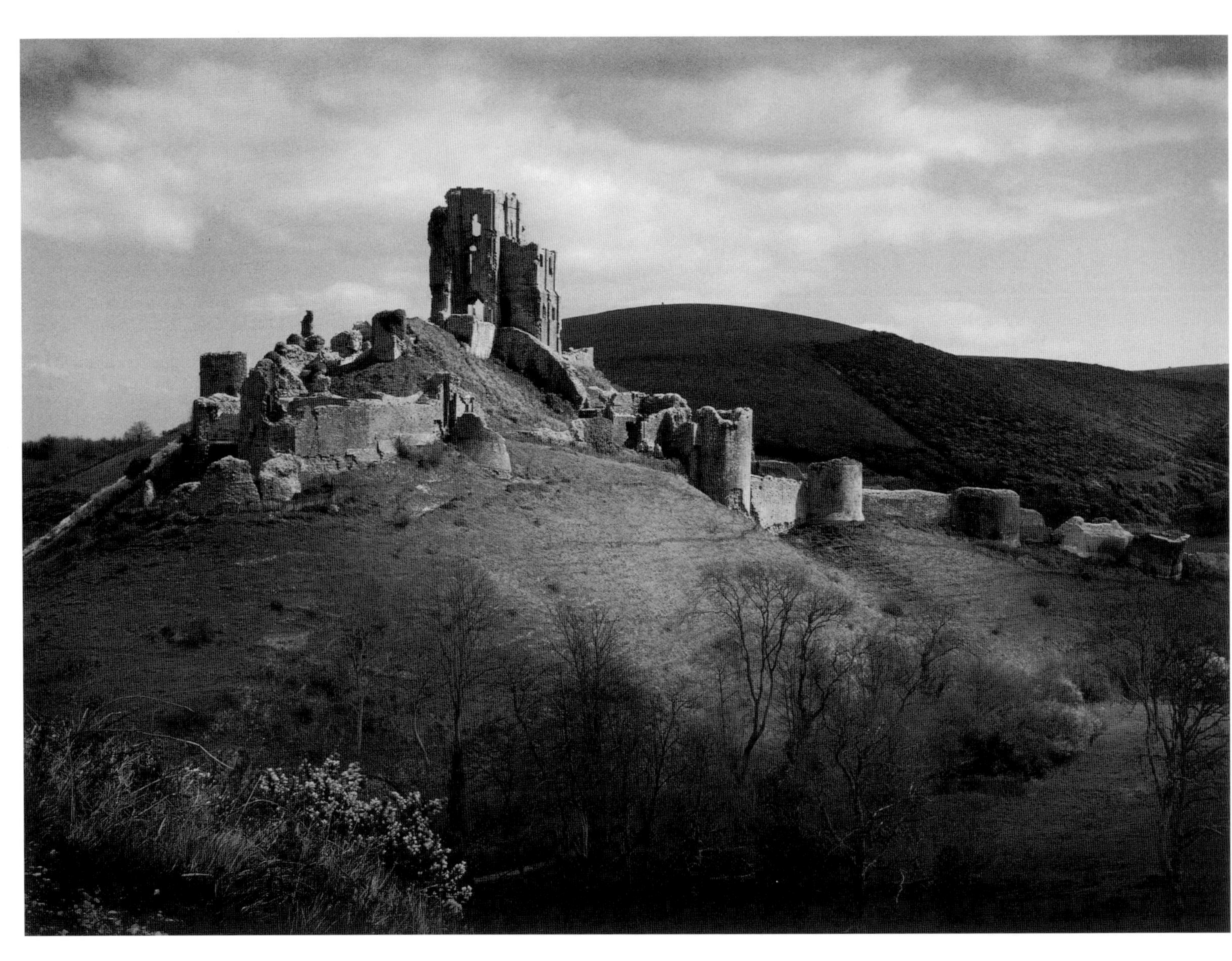

Corfe Castle, Corfe, Dorset by Rob Dyson

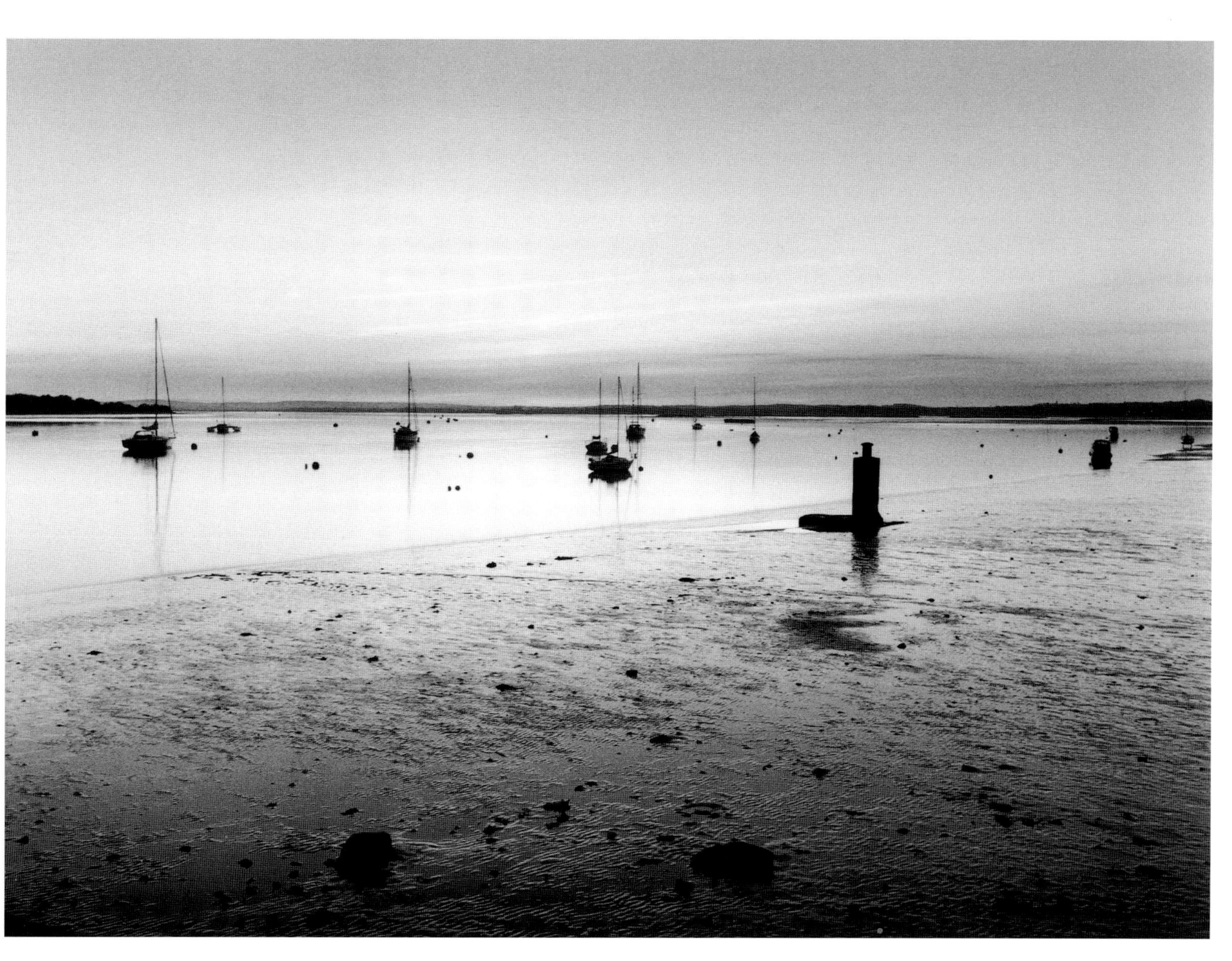

Poole Harbour, Poole, Dorset by Rob Dyson

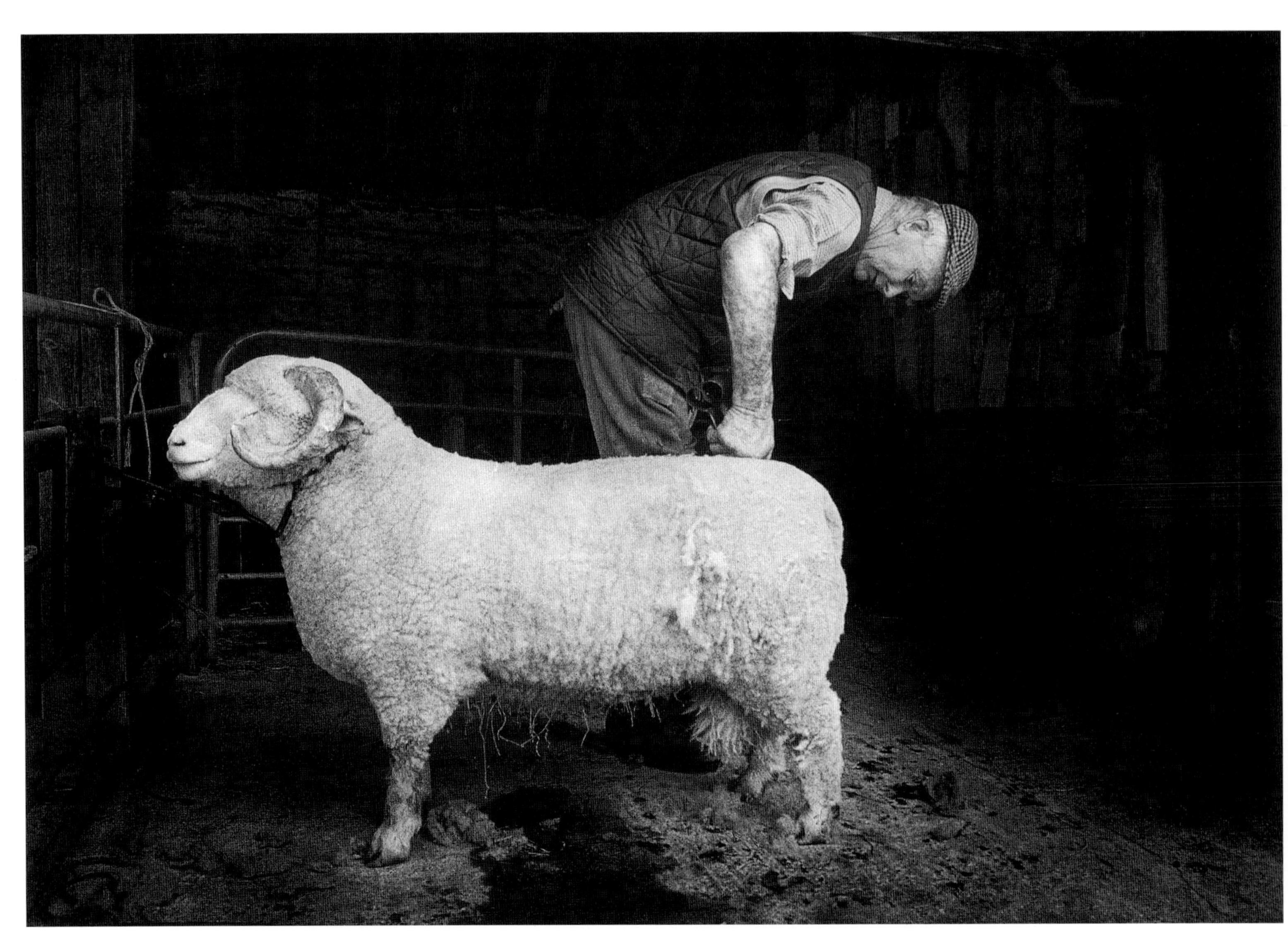

John Randall, Trimming a Dorset Horn Ram, Litton Cheney, Dorset by Pauline Rook

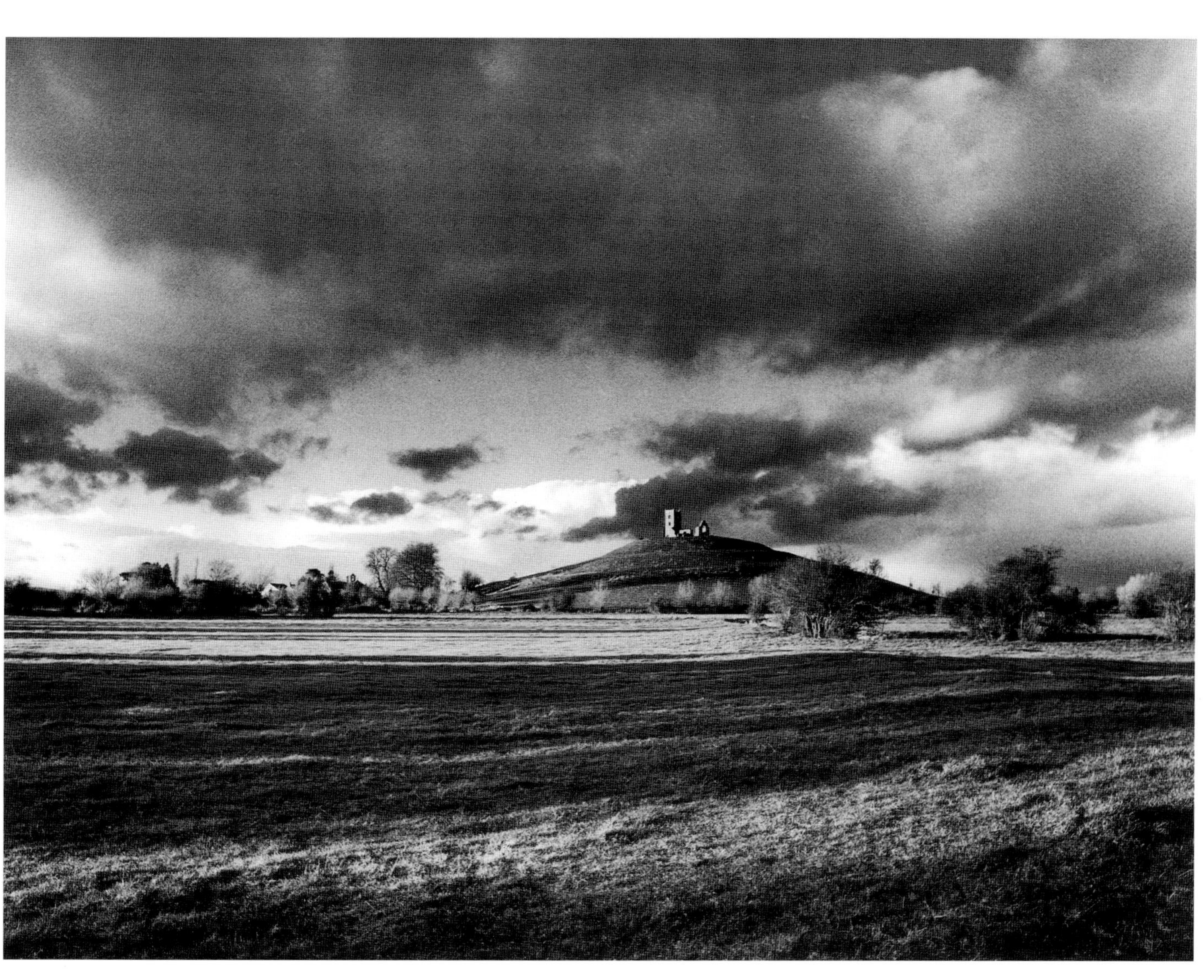

Burrow Mump, Burrowbridge, Somerset Levels, Somerset by Pauline Rook

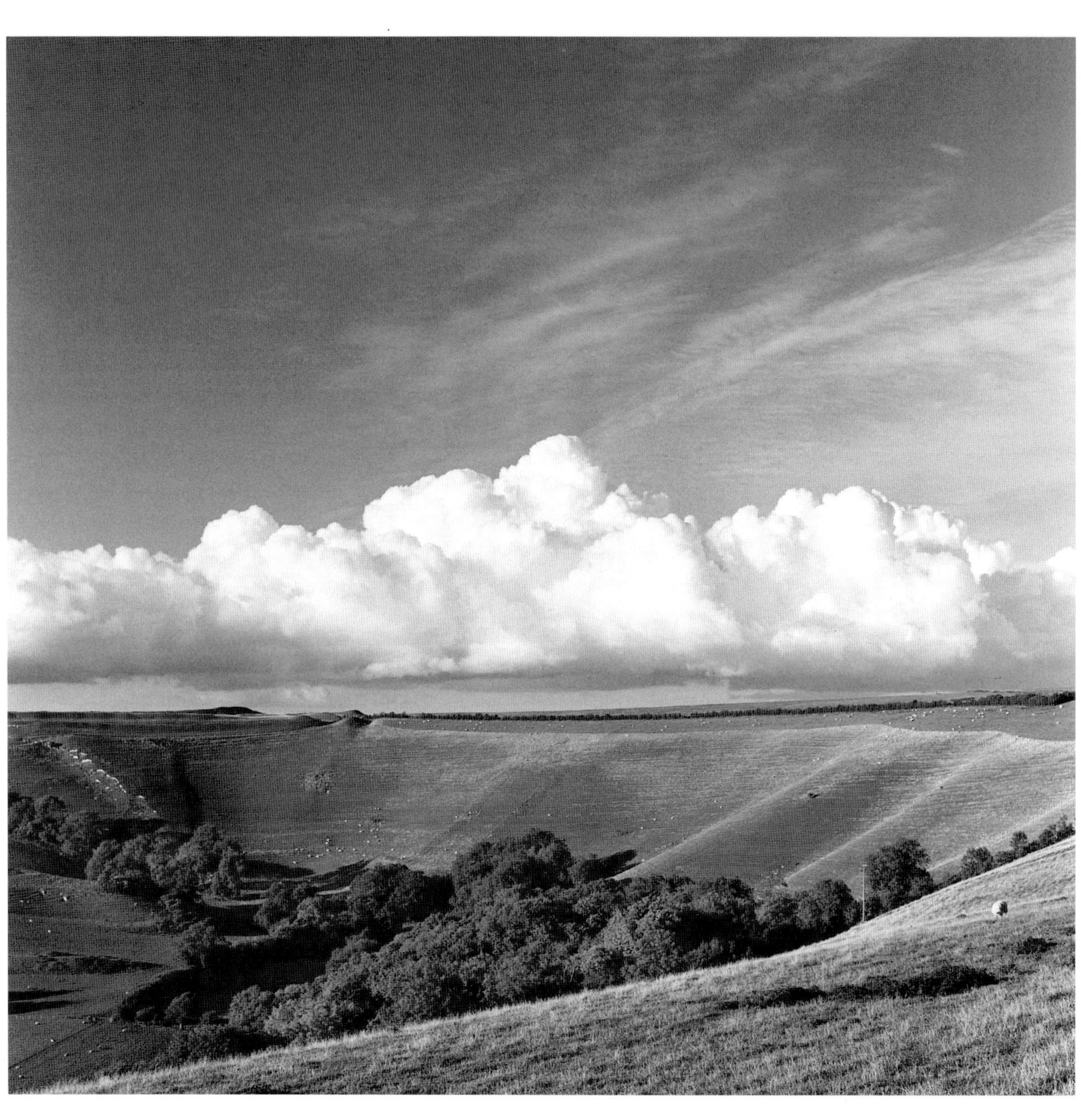

Eggardon Hill, Dorset by Christopher Rimmer

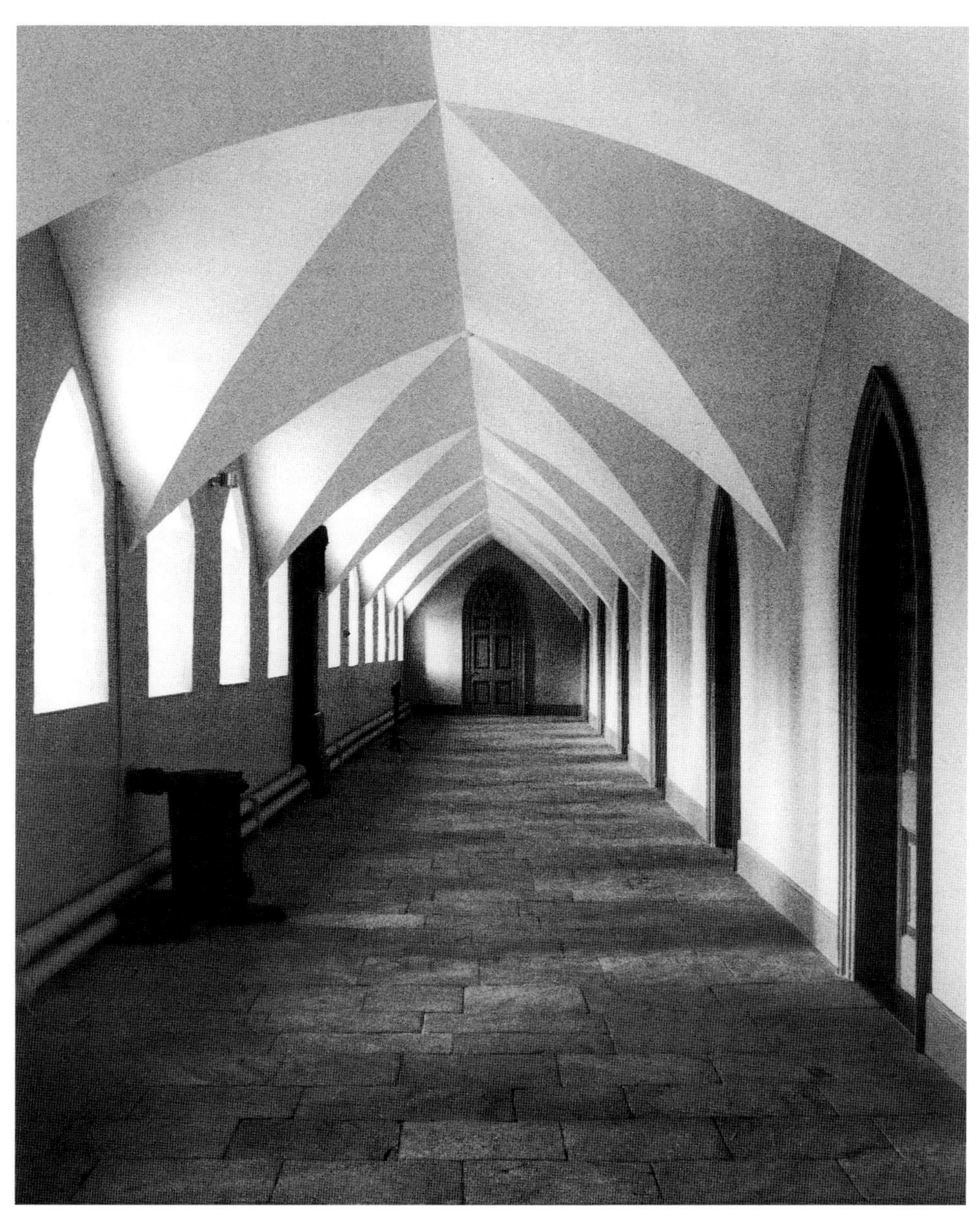

Monks' Walk, Forde Abbey, Dorset by Gerald Singleton

PRODUCTION NOTE

The creative ideas for this book came to me in 1999, and I started compiling the work just over a year before publication. Forty photographers responded to my invitation to submit work, and the final ninety photographs were selected from a total of over one thousand images. The majority of photographs were taken within the past three years; all have been taken within the past eight years. The entire collection of photographs was displayed in an exhibition *Shadows in Time* at The Town Mill Gallery, Lyme Regis, Dorset, in the summer of 2002.

At the outset it was decided that the book would be image-driven, and just include images from the West Country, taken by photographers living and working there. The photographers' ages range from twenty to eighty. Some are in professional practice; others use photography purely as an enjoyable creative art form and all have an absolute passion for the power of the monochrome image. When the ninety photographs were in place, I arranged the facing pages in a complementary way. The choice of image would be determined by visual consideration rather than prescriptive in terms of geographical locations.

Finally, graphics and layout were decided. My choice of typeface was Bembo, a true classic, which is nearly five hundred years old. It was designed by the Venetian printer Aldus Manutius, and dates back to the Italian Renaissance of the 15th and 16th centuries. Manutius had a very interesting motto, *festina lente*, or 'make haste slowly', which I think captures the spirit of this design: timelessness.

The book is very much designed on the visual image, and I hope I have been able to do justice to the art and craft of my forty contributors, by presenting their work in an exciting and visually stimulating publication.

REFERENCES

Austen, J. (1970) *Persuasion*, Oxford.

Fowles, J. (1969) *The French Lieutenant's Woman*, Jonathan Cape Ltd.

Fowles, J. (1972) *Crabbing* - unpublished in the UK.

Galvin, P. (1998) *I have Lived with Shades: Poems and Prose by Thomas Hardy*, Ridgeway Publishing.

Hardy, T. (1981) *The Woodlanders*, Penguin.

Hutchings, M. (1963) *Inside Somerset*, Sherborne, The Abbey Press.

Hutchings, M. (1965) *Inside Dorset*, Sherborne, The Abbey Press.

Hutton, G. & Cooke, O. (2001) *English Parish Churches*, Thames & Hudson World of Art.

Hutton, G. & Cooke, O. (2001) *English Parish Churches*, Thames & Hudson World of Art.

James, P.D. (1975) *The Black Tower*, Penguin.

Legg, R. (1990) *Literary Dorset*, Dorset Publishing Company.

Newman, J. & Pevsner, N. (1972) *The Buildings of England, Dorset*, Penguin Books.

Sutherland, P. & Nicholson, A. (1987) *Wetlands: Life in the Somerset Levels*, Michael Joseph London.

Tolhurst, P. (1999) *Wessex A Literary Pilgrimage*, Black Dog Books.

Research: *Dianne Dowling*

TECHNICAL NOTE

All the photographers have received formal training, and around half are Associates of The Royal Photographic Society - Applied and Professional Photography. A wide range of camera systems were used: Nikon, Canon, Olympus, Pentax, Leica in 35mm format; and Mamiya, Bronica and Hasselblad in medium format (6x4.5cm, 6x6cm and 6x7cm). About two-thirds of the images were taken using medium format. Only one photograph, *The Chapter House Steps, Wells Cathedral,* was taken using large format 4x5" Horseman, and one photograph *The Somerset Levels from the Polden Hills*, was taken on a medium format panoramic camera, which was designed and manufactured by the photographer, retired physicist, Richard Lane.

Good practice in photography involves using appropriate camera systems and film stock, hand-held or with tripod. For example, fast film, hand-held was used by Maisie Hill on a medium format twin lens camera; whilst a tripod was essential for the architectural images by Janet Carmichael, which required a long exposure. Camera-shake caused by wind-blow on the hill forts, distracting cloud movement, and tripod settlement on shingle beaches were prevented. Great care was taken in the use of appropriate lighting, whilst harsh and flat lighting was avoided. Consideration was taken to square the film-plane to the subject matter when taking the photographs, such as church interior detail at close range; and to critical edge composition. Cross-lighting was used for the exterior architectural shots, including the north-facing architecture, where possible.

The majority of cameras used were high quality, straight-forward, manual systems, with a range of quality lenses. Lens filters, tripods and cable-releases, and hand-held light meters, were used extensively where appropriate. The film stock used fell broadly into three categories: Agfa Pan APX 25 and APX 100 ISO/ASA, developed in Rodinal; Ilford HP5 mainly rated at 200 ISO/ASA, developed in Aculux; and Kodak T400CN 400 ISO/ASA, using C41 commercial process. Two images were taken using 35mm Kodak Infrared film, *The Broken Cross* and *Young Woman in the Dillington Woodland*. All films were developed with great care, making the necessary adjustments in development time, to ensure optimum quality in terms of density, tonal range and contrast. Both condenser and diffuser enlargers were used.

With regard to exposure, all the photographers used the zone system, and the reciprocity law calculation adjustment when films were exposed under low-light conditions - exposures in excess of half a second.

The use of the zone system and reciprocity law calculation was most important when photographing a diversity of church interiors: wall paintings, stained glass, stone carvings and delicate woodwork, such as the interior architectural images taken by Stan Ashcroft and the Whistler etched glass taken by Pat Garth.

The photographic papers used were, in the main, Ilford Warmtone fibre-based exhibition paper, and Agfa Classic Multigrade fibre-based exhibition paper. All original prints were made on 12x16" paper. A few of the earlier photographs were printed on Agfa Record Rapid fibre-based exhibition paper. All original prints were hand-crafted in the traditional manner in the darkroom by the photographers, using appropriate dodging, burning and post-flashing - all techniques being incremental in one-eighth stops - no two finished prints are the same. The fine printing of the images involved many hours in the darkroom. The prints were developed in Bromophen, fixed in Hypam and selenium-dipped for archival permanence. Print finishing, spotting and mounting in archival systems were undertaken by the photographers. Negatives were referenced, and prints were stored in archival storage systems.

INDEX OF CONTRIBUTORS AND PLATES

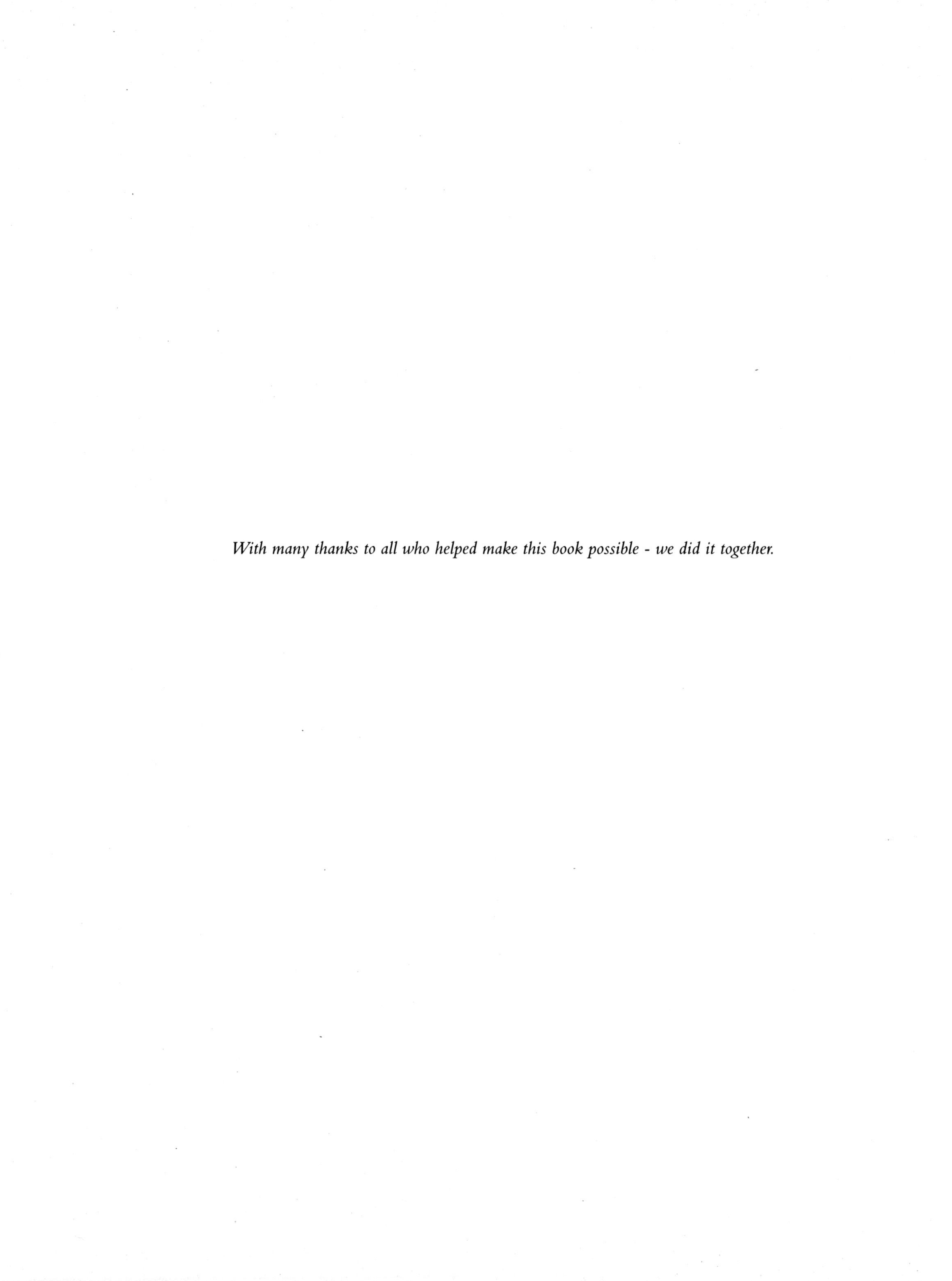

With many thanks to all who helped make this book possible - we did it together.